COOKBOOKS

Presents

85 Fat-Burning Diet Meal Recipes

To Help You Lose Weight Faster and Stay Full Longer

CONTENTS

INTRODUCTION

Eating to lose weight doesn't have to be boring, expensive, tasteless or difficult. Everything you need to make 20/20 Cookbooks' 85 fat-burning recipes can be found at your local supermarket, and there's no need to buy organic or premium brand foods unless you want to. If you stock your pantry with the key foods described below, grocery shopping and meal prep will be a breeze!

Why All Calories are Not Alike:
The Hidden Power of Bioactive Foods

People often say that the formula for weight loss is simple: as long as you take in fewer calories than you expend, it doesn't matter what kind of foods you eat. A calorie is a calorie, they say.

But that's not exactly true.

Some foods have what's known as a *metabolic advantage* and will produce greater weight loss than other foods that have the exact same number of calories.

First of all, there are some foods that reduce the amount of energy (calories) we absorb from what we eat. Studies have shown, for example, that dietary calcium lowers the absorption of fat, and hence calories.

Not only that, but there are also specific foods that pump up our metabolism more than other foods do. Any time we eat, our bodies experience what's known as *diet-induced thermogenesis*—an increase in heat production (and hence calorie-burning) while we digest our food. Depending on the food, this increase can be as much as 10-15% of our calorie intake. Emerging research suggests that choosing foods with a high thermogenic profile, like hot chilis, can lead to greater weight loss.

Lastly, some foods, especially ones rich in fiber, increase our feelings of satiety, or fullness, leading us to eat fewer calories and making us more likely to stick to our diet. Some of them also increase our expenditure of calories or reduce our absorption of them, giving us even more bang for our caloric buck.

All of the recipes in this fat-burning 20/20 cookbook combine foods that emerging research suggests have the metabolic advantages just described:

- **Nuts like Almonds, Pistachios, and Walnuts** are diet powerhouses, combining a high satiety index with poor calorie absorption and strong thermogenic effects. Some studies have also shown that people who include nuts in moderation stick to their diets better than people who don't.

- **Eggs** are a protein shown to promote satiety.

- **Yogurt & Whey** are dairy proteins shown to enhance diet-induced thermogenesis and to encourage feelings of satiety. Yogurt's acidity also leads to higher bioavailability of calcium, which has been linked with reduced fat absorption. In addition, recent studies have proposed that the probiotics in yogurt, by supporting a healthy gut microbiota, may have an added role to play in weight control.

- **Apples** are rich in satiating fiber and have been shown to lead to greater weight loss when compared calorie-for-calorie with other fruits and foods, suggesting that apples possess a particular metabolic advantage that isn't yet fully understood.

- **Leafy Greens**, when consumed as part of a meal, have been shown to lead to a reduced overall calorie consumption and enhanced feelings of fullness.

- **Rye and Other Whole Grains** promote feelings of satiety.

- **Olive Oil** appears from preliminary research to have an even higher diet-induced thermogenesis effect than dairy products.

- **Coconut Oil** is a medium-chain triglyceride shown in studies to have weight-loss-enhancing effects, most likely via its stimulation of both fat oxidation and energy expenditure.

- **Raisins and Other Dried Fruits** like prunes are rich in dietary fiber and have been shown to reduce food intake and increase satiety.

- **Fish like Cod, and Other Seafood**, when included as a regular part of a person's diet, have been shown to lead to more weight loss than seafood-free diets containing the same number of calories.

- **Legumes like Chickpeas, Beans, Lentils, and Peanuts** are high in protein and fiber and promote satiety and, according to at least one case study, reduce overall food consumption.

- **Seasonings like Dijon Mustard and Hot Chili Peppers**, recent studies suggest, may reduce calorie absorption and increase diet-induced thermogenesis.

- Although **green tea** is not used an ingredient in any recipes here, its caffeine and catechin content is believed to increase both thermogenesis and fat oxidation, making it an excellent beverage choice.

Important Notes on Salt and Sugar

Lately, there has been an increasing call for recognizing the dangers of salt and sugar in the diet. Both have been likened to addictions and implicated in the global obesity epidemic. Salt consumption has long been recognized as a significant factor in the development of cardiovascular disease but is only now beginning to be seen as a potential, independent risk factor for weight gain and obesity as well.

The recipes in this book, therefore, do not call for the addition of any salt or sugar (or refined carbohydrates in general) and rely primarily on whole foods in their natural state. Flavorful herbs and other seasonings are used to enhance the taste of the meals, but for those new to a low-salt diet, many of the recipes will likely seem bland. The good news is that studies have shown that, over time, people who adopt and stick to a lower sodium diet will learn not only to tolerate but to prefer less salt in their food.

Speak to your doctor before starting this or any diet about your individual nutritional needs and goals.

Selected References

Thermogenesis and Satiety

Feinman RD and Fine EJ. "'A calorie is a calorie' violates the second law of thermodynamics. *Nutr J.* 2004 Jul 28; 3: 9.

Rebello CJ et al. "Dietary strategies to increase satiety." *Adv Food Nutr Res.* 2013; 69: 105-82.

Astrup A et al. "Can bioactive foods affect obesity?" *Ann N Y Acad Sci.* 2010 Mar; 1190: 25-41.

Rebello C, Greenway FL, and Dhurandhar NV. "Functional foods to promote weight loss and satiety." *Curr Opin Clin Nutr Metab Care.* 2014 Nov; 17(6): 596-604.

Nuts like Almonds, Pistachios, and Walnuts

Mattes RD and Dreher ML. "Nuts and healthy body weight maintenance mechanisms." *Asia Pac J Clin Nutr*. 2010; 19(1): 137-41.

Eggs

Rebello C, Greenway FL, and Dhurandhar NV. "Functional foods to promote weight loss and satiety." *Curr Opin Clin Nutr Metab Care*. 2014 Nov; 17(6): 596-604.

Yogurt & Whey

Bendtsen LQ et al. "Effect of dairy proteins on appetite, energy expenditure, body weight, and composition: a review of the evidence from controlled clinical trials." *Adv Nutr*. 2013 Jul 1; 4(4): 418-38.

Eales J et al. "Is consuming yoghurt associated with weight management outcomes? Results from a systematic review." *Int J Obes (Lond)*. 2015 Oct 7.

Jacques PF and Wang H. "Yogurt and weight management." *Am J Clin Nutr*. 2014 May; 99 (5 Suppl): 1229S-34S.

Apples & Other Fruits

Hyson DA. "A comprehensive review of apples and apple components and their relationship to human health." *Adv Nutr*. 2011 Sep; 2(5): 408-20.

Leafy Greens & Other Vegetables

McGraw, Dr. Phil. *The 20/20 Diet: Turn Your Weight Loss Vision Into Reality*. Bird Street Books, 2015.

Rye and Other Whole Grains

Rebello C, Greenway FL, and Dhurandhar NV. "Functional foods to promote weight loss and satiety." *Curr Opin Clin Nutr Metab Care*. 2014 Nov; 17(6): 596-604.

Olive Oil

Austel A et al. "Weight loss with a modified Mediterranean-type diet using fat modification: a randomized controlled trial." *Eur J Clin Nutr*. 2015 Aug; 69(8): 878-84.

Coconut Oil

St-Onge MP et al. "Medium-chain triglycerides increase energy expenditure and decrease adiposity in overweight men." *Obes Res.* 2003 Mar; 11(3): 395-402.

Raisins and Other Dried Fruits

Anderson JW and Waters AR. "Raisin consumption by humans: effects on glycemia and insulinemia and cardiovascular risk factors." *J Food Sci.* 2013 Jun; 78 Suppl 1: A11-7.

Fish like Cod, and Other Seafood

Ramel A, Jonsdottir MT, and Thorsdottir I. "Consumption of cod and weight loss in young overweight and obese adults on an energy reduced diet for 8-weeks." *Nutr Metab Cardiovasc Dis.* 2009 Dec; 19(10): 690-6.

Thorsdottir I et al. "Randomized trial of weight-loss-diets for young adults varying in fish and fish oil content." *Int J Obes (Lond).* 2007 Oct; 31(10): 1560-6.

Legumes like Chickpeas, Beans and Lentils

McCrory MA et al. "Pulse consumption, satiety, and weight management." *Adv Nutr.* 2010 Nov; 1(1): 17-30.

Green Tea

Türközü D and Acar Tek N. "A Minireview of Effects of Green Tea on Energy Expenditure." *Crit Rev Food Sci Nutr.* 2015 Jun 19.

Seasonings

Gregersen NT et al. "Acute effects of mustard, horseradish, black pepper and ginger on energy expenditure, appetite, ad libitum energy intake and energy balance in human subjects." *Br J Nutr.* 2013 Feb 14; 109(3): 556-63.

Salt

Grimes CA et al. "Dietary salt intake, sugar-sweetened beverage consumption, and obesity risk." *Pediatrics.* 2013 Jan; 131(1): 14-21.

Ma Y, He FJ, and MacGregor GA. "High salt intake: independent risk factor for obesity?" *Hypertension.* 2015 Oct; 66(4): 843-9.

Tekol Y. "Salt addiction: a different kind of drug addiction." *Med Hypotheses.* 2006; 67(5): 1233-4.

Sugar

Ifland JR et al. "Refined food addiction: a classic substance use disorder." *Med Hypotheses.* 2009 May; 72(5): 518-26.

LUNCH AND DINNER RECIPES

BAKED HADDOCK AND MUSHROOM OPEN-FACED SANDWICH

Makes 2 servings

INGREDIENTS

Proteins:

haddock, 8 oz

Vegetables and Fruits:

mushrooms, 3 oz, button, chopped
shallots, 1 shallot, minced
red leaf lettuce, 2 handfuls
lemons, 1/2 lemon, cut into wedges

Starch:

bread, whole grain rye, 2 pieces

Fats:

olive oil, extra virgin, 4 tsp

Seasonings:

garlic, 2 cloves, minced
pepper, black, 1/4 tsp
chili powder, chipotle, 1/8 tsp
parsley, 4 sprigs

INSTRUCTIONS

1. Heat olive oil in a skillet over medium heat. Add mushrooms and shallots. Cook for 5 minutes or until tender. Add garlic and cook for another minute.

2. Season the haddock with black pepper and chili powder.

3. Cover a baking dish with nonstick foil or parchment paper. Place the fish in the dish, then top with the mushroom shallot mixture and finally the parsley.

4. Bake, covered, for 30-35 minutes, until the fish is flaky and tender.

5. Top each piece of rye bread with red leaf lettuce. Place the fish and toppings on the lettuce and serve with lemon wedges on the side.

BLACK BEAN AND AVOCADO TORTILLAS

Makes 2 servings

INGREDIENTS

Proteins:

beans, 2/3 cup, black, canned, reduced sodium, drained, rinsed
yogurt, Greek, plain, nonfat, 3 oz (about 1/3 cup)

Vegetables and Fruits:

tomatoes, 1 cup, diced
jalapeno peppers, 1/2 small, seeds removed, diced finely
limes, 2 limes, small

Starch:

corn tortillas, whole grain, 4 tortillas

Fats:

avocado, 1/2 avocado, peeled and pitted
olive oil, extra virgin, 1/2 tsp

Seasonings:

garlic, 2 cloves, minced
cumin, 1 tsp
chili powder, chipotle, 1/2 tsp
scallions, 1 bunch, sliced
cilantro, 1 tbsp, fresh, chopped

INSTRUCTIONS

1. Slice avocado and toss with the juice from 1/2 lime. Set aside.

2. Over medium-high heat in a medium saucepan, heat olive oil. Saute garlic for 1 minute. Add beans, tomatoes, jalapeno pepper, cumin, and chili powder. Reduce heat to simmering and cook for 10 minutes.

3. Meanwhile, warm tortillas by piling them in a stack, wrapping the stack with aluminum foil, and placing in an oven preheated to 375 for 10-15 minutes.

4. Spoon bean mixture into tortillas and top with avocado, scallions, Greek yogurt, and cilantro.

BLACK BEAN CAKES

Makes 2 servings

INGREDIENTS

Proteins:

beans, 1 cup, black, canned, reduced sodium, drained, rinsed

Vegetables and Fruits:

limes, 1 small lime
baby mixed greens, 2 cups

Starch:

rye flakes, whole grain, 1/4 cup

Fats:

olive oil, extra virgin, 4 tsp

Seasonings:

scallions, 2 tbsp, chopped finely
cilantro, 1 tbsp, fresh, chopped
cumin, 1/2 tsp
pepper, crushed red, 1/8 tsp
garlic, 1 clove, minced
dijon mustard, 1/4 tsp
pepper, black, 1/4 tsp

INSTRUCTIONS

1. Preheat oven to 350 degrees F. Toast rye flakes on a baking sheet for 5 minutes or until slightly brown.

2. Mash black beans using a ricer, food processor, or blender. In a medium bowl, combine black beans, rye flakes, scallions, cilantro, cumin, crushed red pepper, and garlic.

3. Form black bean mixture into 2 cakes of equal size. Over medium-high heat in a medium skillet, heat 2 tsp olive oil. Add the patties and cook for 3 minutes on each side.

4. Combine 2 tsp olive oil with 1-1/2 tsp fresh lime juice, dijon mustard, and black pepper. Toss with baby greens.

BLACK BEAN PASTA SALAD

Makes 2 servings

INGREDIENTS

Proteins:

> **beans**, 1 cup, black, canned, reduced sodium, drained, rinsed

Vegetables and Fruits:

> **tomatoes**, 1 cup, grape, halved
> **cucumbers**, 1 small, diced
> **jalapeno peppers**, 1/4 seeded, minced
> **limes**, 1 small

Starch:

> **pasta, whole grain**, 1/2 cup, rotini, dry, uncooked

Fats:

> **avocado**, 1/2 avocado, peeled, diced

Seasonings:

> **scallions**, 2 tbsp, sliced
> **cilantro**, 1 tbsp, chopped
> **vinegar, cider**, 1 tbsp
> **dijon mustard**, 1 tsp
> **garlic powder**, 1/2 tsp
> **pepper, black**, 1/4 tsp

INSTRUCTIONS

1. Cook pasta in boiling water until al dente, about 9-11 minutes. Drain and cool.

2. In a large bowl, combine the beans, tomatoes, cucumbers, jalapeno pepper, avocado, scallions, and cilantro.

3. Cut lime in half. Zest and juice one half. In a small bowl, combine the lime zest and juice with the vinegar, dijon mustard, garlic powder, and black pepper.

4. Add pasta and dressing to bean mixture.

5. Cut remaining 1/2 lime in half and serve as a garnish.

BLACK BEANS AND RICE

Makes 2 servings

INGREDIENTS

Proteins:

beans, 1 cup, black, canned, reduced sodium, drained, rinsed

Vegetables and Fruits:

onion, 1 small, diced
bell peppers, 1 small, red, seeded and diced

Starch:

rice, whole grain brown or wild, 1/4 cup, raw, uncooked

Fats:

olive oil, extra virgin, 4 tsp

Seasonings:

garlic, 2 cloves, minced
water, 1/4 cup
dijon mustard, 1 tsp
chili powder, chipotle, 1/2 tsp
cumin, 1/4 tsp, ground
oregano, 1/4 tsp, dried
coriander seed, 1/4 tsp, ground
pepper, crushed red, 1/8 tsp

INSTRUCTIONS

1. Prepare whole-grain or wild rice according to package directions.

2. While the rice cooks, heat olive oil in a medium saucepan over medium-high heat. Add onion and bell pepper. Cook, stirring occasionally, until tender, about 8 minutes. Add garlic and continue cooking for one minute.

3. Add water, dijon mustard, chili powder, cumin, oregano, coriander, crushed red pepper, and beans.

4. Bring to a boil, then reduce to simmer. Cover and cook for 10 minutes. Serve atop the rice.

BLACKENED CATFISH WITH REMOULADE AND ROASTED CORN ON THE COB

Makes 2 servings

INGREDIENTS

Proteins:

> **catfish**, 6 oz, fillet
> **yogurt, Greek**, plain, nonfat, 1/4 cup

Vegetables and Fruits:

> **shallots**, 1 tbsp, chopped very finely
> **pickles, gherkin**, 1 tbsp, chopped
> **romaine**, 6 hearts

Starch:

> **corn**, 1 large ear (8-9" long), cleaned and cut in half (or 2 frozen mini ears)

Fats:

> **olive oil**, extra virgin, 4 tsp

Seasonings:

> **pepper, black**, 1-1/4 tsp
> **garlic**, 2 cloves, minced
> **thyme**, 1-1/2 tsp
> **pepper, cayenne**, 1-1/4 tsp, divided
> **parsley**, 1 tbsp, fresh, chopped

INSTRUCTIONS

1. In a small bowl, combine 1 tsp black pepper, garlic, shallots, thyme, and 1 tsp of the cayenne pepper. Rub onto both sides of the catfish.

2. Prepare the remoulade by combining the pickle, yogurt, parsley, 1/4 tsp of cayenne pepper, and 1/4 tsp black pepper in a small bowl.

3. Bring a large pot of water to boiling. Place the corn pieces in the water and cook for about 10 minutes, or until the corn is tender.

4. Heat a cast iron skillet over medium heat. Add olive oil to the skillet. Cook catfish for 4 minutes on the first side, then flip over and cook for about 4 more minutes, until the fish flakes easily with a fork.

5. Serve the catfish and corn over a bed of romaine hearts with the remoulade.

BREADED COD WITH WILTED GREENS

Makes 2 servings

INGREDIENTS

Proteins:

cod, 8 oz

Vegetables and Fruits:

lemons, 1 lemon, cut into wedges
endive, 3/4 cup, roughly chopped
onion, 1/4 cup, red, diced finely

Starch:

bread, whole grain rye, 2 slices

Fats:

olive oil, extra virgin, 4 tsp

Seasonings:

pepper, cayenne, 1/2 tsp
parsley, 1/4 cup
dijon mustard, 2 tbsp
pepper, black, 1/4 tsp

INSTRUCTIONS

1. Heat oven to 250 degrees F. Place bread slices directly on oven rack to dry out, about 1 hour. Remove from the oven and let cool. Use a food processor or blender to chop bread slices into tiny cubes (or tear by hand)

2. In a small bowl, mix the cayenne pepper and parsley with dijon mustard. Brush the mustard mixture onto the top side of the cod. Sprinkle the bread crumbs evenly on top of the mustard.

3. Preheat broiler.

4. Drizzle a nonstick baking sheet with 2 tsp of the olive oil. Place the fish, bread crumb side up, onto the tray, and position about 6" below the broiler element. Cook for about 6-7 minutes so that the topping browns and the fish just cooks through.

5. While the fish is cooking, heat the remaining 2 tsp of olive oil in a large saute pan. Add the onions and saute for about 8 minutes until softened and browned. Add the endive and black pepper and cook for a few minutes until the greens are wilted.

6. Serve fish and endive with lemon wedges.

CATFISH CEVICHE WITH SWEET POTATO WEDGES

Makes 2 servings

INGREDIENTS

Proteins:

catfish, 8 oz, fillet, diced

Vegetables and Fruits:

limes, 1 lime, juiced and zested
grapefruit, 1/2 grapefruit, juiced and zested
tomatoes, 1 small, diced
jalapeno peppers, 1/2 minced, seeds removed

Starch:

sweet potatoes, 1 small sweet potato, 5" long

Fats:

avocado, 1/4 avocado, peeled and diced
olive oil, extra virgin, 2 tsp

Seasonings:

garlic, 2 cloves, minced
cilantro, 1/2 tbsp, chopped
cumin, 1/4 tsp
paprika, 1/2 tsp

INSTRUCTIONS

1. Combine the catfish, 1/2 tsp lime zest, 1/2 tsp grapefruit zest, and all of the lime and grapefruit juice in a large plastic bag or covered bowl. Refrigerate for 6 hours, turning twice.

2. Remove the fish from the marinade and combine it in a medium bowl with the tomato, jalapeno, avocado, cilantro, cumin, and 1 tsp of olive oil.

3. Refrigerate, covered, for at least half an hour.

4. One hour prior to serving, preheat oven to 350 degrees F.

5. Clean, peel, and slice the sweet potato lengthwise into quarters. Toss with 1 remaining tsp of olive oil and dust evenly with paprika.

6. Bake sweet potatoes on a tray lined with parchment paper or nonstick aluminum foil for 50 minutes. Serve warm or at room temperature with the ceviche.

CATFISH GUMBO

Makes 2 servings

INGREDIENTS

Proteins:

catfish, 8 oz, fillet

Vegetables and Fruits:

onion, 1 small, diced
celery, 1/3 cup, diced
bell peppers, 1/2 green, diced finely
tomatoes, 1 cup, diced
tomato sauce, all natural, 1/4 cup
okra, 1/2 cup, diced, frozen

Starch:

rice, whole grain brown or wild, 1/3 cup, dry measure, prepared with water according to package directions

Fats:

olive oil, extra virgin, 4 tsp

Seasonings:

pepper, black, 1/4 tsp
cajun seasoning, 3/4 tsp
bay leaf, 1 bay leaf, chopped finely
garlic, 3 cloves
dijon mustard, 1/2 tsp
vegetable broth, low sodium, 1/2 cup

INSTRUCTIONS

1. In a small bowl, mix the black pepper, cajun seasoning, and bay leaf.

2. Meanwhile, in a large saucepan, heat the olive oil over medium heat. Add the onions, celery, and green peppers and cook until softened and slightly browned, about 8 minutes. Add the garlic and continue cooking for another minute.

3. Stir in the dijon mustard, vegetable broth, tomatoes, tomato sauce, and okra. Then add the cajun seasoning mixture and stir well.

4. Bring the pot to a boil and then reduce to simmering. Cook for 30 minutes.

5. Add the catfish and stir. Cover and simmer for an additional 20 minutes. Serve over prepared rice.

CHEESE- AND TURKEY-FILLED SPAGHETTI SQUASH BOATS

Makes 2 servings

INGREDIENTS

Proteins:

turkey, ground, extra lean, 4 oz
cottage cheese, lowfat or nonfat, 1/2 cup

Vegetables and Fruits:

tomato sauce, all natural, 3/4 cup
spaghetti squash, 1 small
spinach, shredded, 2 cups

Starch:

corn, 2/3 cup, kernels, frozen

Fats:

olive oil, extra virgin, 4 tsp

Seasonings:

Italian herb seasoning, salt free, dried, 1 tbsp
garlic, 3 cloves, minced

INSTRUCTIONS

1. Preheat oven to 350. Cut the spaghetti squash in half. Remove seeds. Place the two halves with the cut side facing up on a baking sheet lined with nonstick aluminum foil. Bake for 50 minutes, then let stand for 10 minutes. Scrape squash strands out carefully and set aside in a medium bowl.

2. In a small bowl, mix the tomato sauce with the Italian herb seasoning. Over medium-high heat in a large skillet, heat 2 tsp olive oil. Add garlic and cook for 30 seconds. Add spinach and stir until wilted, about 1 minute. Remove from heat.

3. Add the spinach mixture and the cottage cheese to the bowl containing the squash strands.

4. Heat remaining 2 tsp olive oil in the large skillet over medium-high heat. Add the ground turkey. Cook, stirring, for 4 minutes or until browned. Add the seasoned tomato sauce and corn. Bring to boil, then reduce to simmering. Cook for 4 minutes, then remove from heat. Gently fold in the spinach, squash, and cottage cheese mixture.

5. Remove squash from the oven, then increase temperature to 425 degrees F. Top squash halves evenly with the turkey-squash mixture. Bake for 20 minutes, then let stand for 10 minutes before serving.

CHICKEN AND LEEK STEW

Makes 2 servings

INGREDIENTS

Proteins:

chicken breast, boneless, skinless, 8 oz, cut into bite-sized pieces

Vegetables and Fruits:

carrots, 1 cup, peeled and sliced
leeks, 1 leek, cleaned well, trimmed of tough green tips, and sliced thinly
mushrooms, 1 cup, fresh, sliced
celery, 2 stalks, sliced

Starch:

barley, 1/4 cup, whole grain, raw, uncooked

Fats:

olive oil, extra virgin, 4 tsp

Seasonings:

vegetable broth, low sodium, 1 cup
dijon mustard, 1 tsp
pepper, black, 1/4 tsp

INSTRUCTIONS

1. Over medium-high heat in a medium stock pot, heat olive oil. Add carrots, leeks, mushrooms, and celery and cook, stirring frequently, for 8 minutes until tender.

2. Add chicken, barley, vegetable broth, dijon mustard, and black pepper. Bring to a boil, then reduce to simmer. Continue cooking until the chicken is no longer pink inside and the barley is tender, about 30 minutes.

CHICKEN AND SWEET POTATO STEW

Makes 2 servings

INGREDIENTS

Proteins:

chicken breast, boneless, skinless, 8 oz, cut into bite-sized chunks

Vegetables and Fruits:

beets, 1 small, peeled and diced
carrots, 1 small, peeled and diced
celery, 1 stalk, diced
onion, 1 small, peeled and diced
endive, 1 cup, shredded

Starch:

sweet potatoes, 1 small, 5" long, scrubbed and cubed

Fats:

olive oil, extra virgin, 4 tsp

Seasonings:

vegetable broth, low sodium, 2 cups (more if needed)
thyme, 1/2 tsp
bay leaf, 1 leaf, whole

INSTRUCTIONS

1. Over medium-high heat in a medium pot, heat the olive oil. Cook the chicken, stirring frequently, until browned on all sides, about 5 minutes.

2. Add the beet, carrot, celery, onion, endive, sweet potato, thyme, and bay leaf. Pour enough vegetable broth in to cover.

3. Bring to a boil, then reduce to simmering and cook for 3 hours until the sweet potatoes and other vegetables are soft.

4. Remove bay leaf and serve.

CHICKEN ROULADE WITH ALMOND CRUST AND SPINACH POTATO STUFFING

Makes 2 servings

INGREDIENTS

Proteins:

chicken breast, boneless, skinless, 6 oz
cottage cheese, lowfat or nonfat, 1/4 cup

Vegetables and Fruits:

baby spinach, 2 cups

Starch:

potatoes, skin on, 1 small

Fats:

almonds, 2 tbsp
olive oil, extra virgin, 2 tsp

Seasonings:

garlic powder, 1 tsp
pepper, black, 1/4 tsp
pepper, cayenne, 1/4 tsp

INSTRUCTIONS

1. Scrub potato skin, cut potato in half, and boil in water until tender, about 15-20 minutes. Mash with a ricer or potato masher. Allow to cool. Microwave spinach in a large bowl for 3 minutes on high, or until wilted. Let cool.

2. Preheat oven to 375 degrees F. Place chicken breast between two sheets of plastic wrap. Pound with a meat tenderizer until 1/4" thin. Divide into two equal-sized portions.

3. Pulverize almonds in a food processor, or crush by placing in a plastic bag and using a rolling pin.

4. In a medium bowl, combine cottage cheese, baby spinach, and mashed potatoes with the garlic powder and black and cayenne peppers. Mix well, then spoon onto centers of chicken breasts.

5. Roll up chicken breasts tightly and place on a baking sheet lined with nonstick aluminum foil. Use toothpicks to secure. Brush top side of breasts with olive oil. Press almonds onto exposed parts of breasts.

6. Bake for 35 minutes, or just until the chicken is cooked through with no pinkness remaining.

CHICKEN WITH CASHEWS AND RICE PILAF

Makes 2 servings

INGREDIENTS

Proteins:

chicken breast, boneless, skinless, 8 oz, cut into bite-sized pieces

Vegetables and Fruits:

sugar snap peas, 1 cup, fresh
plums, dried (prunes), 1/4 cup

Starch:

rice, whole grain brown or wild, 1/2 cup, raw, uncooked

Fats:

olive oil, extra virgin, 2 tsp
cashews, 2 tbsp, chopped

Seasonings:

garlic, 4 cloves, minced
ginger, 2 pieces, 1" long, peeled and minced
scallions, 8 scallions, sliced
vinegar, red wine, 2 tbsp
vegetable broth, low sodium, 3/4 cup

INSTRUCTIONS

1. In a resealable plastic bag or covered bowl, combine the garlic with one of the ginger pieces, half of the scallions, and the vinegar. Add the chicken pieces and allow to marinate in the refrigerator for 30 minutes.

2. Prepare the rice pilaf. Over medium-high heat in a small stockpot, heat 1/2 tsp olive oil. Add the other half of the scallions and the remaining ginger piece and saute, stirring, 2 minutes. Add the vegetable broth, dried plums, and rice and bring to a boil. Reduce to simmering and cover. Cook until the liquid is absorbed and the rice is tender, about 35 minutes. Let the rice stand, covered.

3. Over medium-high heat in a large skillet, heat the remaining 1-1/2 tsp olive oil. Add the chicken pieces and saute for 3 minutes, or until the chicken turns opaque throughout. Add the sugar snap peas and saute for about 2 more minutes, until the peas are crisp-tender.

4. Serve chicken and peas over the rice pilaf. Sprinkle with cashews.

CHICKEN WITH PENNE PASTA AND ASPARAGUS

Makes 2 servings

INGREDIENTS

Proteins:

> **chicken breast**, boneless, skinless, 8 oz, cut into 1" chunks

Vegetables and Fruits:

> **asparagus**, 8 large spears, trimmed and cut into 1" strips
> **baby spinach**, 1 cup, shredded

Starch:

> **pasta, whole grain**, 2/3 cup, dry, uncooked, penne

Fats:

> **olive oil, extra virgin**, 2 tsp

Seasonings:

> **garlic**, 2 cloves, minced
> **pepper, black**, 1/2 tsp
> **vegetable broth**, low sodium, 1/2 cup

INSTRUCTIONS

1. Cook pasta in a large pot of boiling water about 8-10 minutes, or until al dente. Drain and set aside.

2. Heat a skillet over medium heat. Add olive oil and allow to come to temperature. Add chicken pieces, garlic, and 1/4 tsp black pepper. Cook, stirring occasionally, until the chicken is browned and cooked through. To check for doneness, poke chicken with a fork to make sure juices run clear. Remove chicken and set aside.

3. Add vegetable broth to the skillet. Add asparagus, shredded spinach, and 1/4 tsp black pepper. Cover and allow asparagus to cook for 5-10 minutes, or until tender. Add the chicken and pasta to the skillet and continue cooking until rewarmed.

CHICKPEA AND POTATO STEW

Makes 2 servings

INGREDIENTS

Proteins:

chickpeas, canned (low sodium), 8 oz, canned, rinsed and drained

Vegetables and Fruits:

onion, 1 small, chopped
tomatoes, 1 medium, cubed

Starch:

potatoes, skin on, 1 small, cubed

Fats:

olive oil, extra virgin, 4 tsp

Seasonings:

cumin, 1/2 tsp
garlic, 3 cloves, minced
coriander seed, 1/2 tsp, ground
vegetable broth, low sodium, 1 cup
pepper, black, 1/4 tsp
cilantro, 1 tbsp, fresh, minced

INSTRUCTIONS

1. In a large saucepan over medium heat, saute cumin in olive oil for 10 seconds. Add the onion and continue to cook until browned, about 8 minutes. Add the garlic and coriander and cook for another minute.

2. Add the vegetable broth, chickpeas, potato, pepper, and 1 tsp cilantro and bring to a boil. Reduce to simmering, cover, and cook until the potato is tender, about 15 minutes.

3. Add the tomato the the stew and simmer about 5 more minutes. Garnish stew with remaining cilantro.

CHICKPEA AND ROASTED RED PEPPER SALAD

Makes 2 servings

INGREDIENTS

Proteins:

chickpeas, canned (low sodium), 1 cup, drained and rinsed

Vegetables and Fruits:

bell peppers, 1 small, red
arugula, 1 cup, baby

Starch:

rye crisps, whole grain, 4 crisps

Fats:

olive oil, extra virgin, 1 tsp
olives, 6 olives, pitted and halved

Seasonings:

vinegar, balsamic, 2 tsp
dijon mustard, 1/4 tsp
pepper, black, 1/4

INSTRUCTIONS

1. Preheat oven to 500 degrees F. Place the whole red pepper on a baking sheet. Cook for 30-45 minutes, until the pepper is charred and fully wrinkled, turning twice. Remove from pan and let cool.

2. Rub the skin from the pepper with fingers. Remove stem and seeds. Slice into strips 1/2" wide.

3. In a medium bowl, mix together olive oil, vinegar, dijon mustard, and black pepper. Fold in the baby arugula, chickpeas, and roasted red peppers. Sprinkle with olives and serve with rye crisps.

CHICKPEA AND SWEET POTATO MASALA

Makes 2 servings

INGREDIENTS

Proteins:

chickpeas, canned (low sodium), 8 oz, drained and rinsed

Vegetables and Fruits:

onion, 1 small, diced
tomatoes, 1 medium, chopped

Starch:

sweet potatoes, 1 small (5" long)

Fats:

coconut oil, 4 tsp

Seasonings:

ginger, 1" piece, peeled and minced
garlic, 2 cloves, minced
curry powder, 1/2 tsp
cumin, 1/2 tsp
coriander seed, 1/2 tsp
garam masala, 1/4 tsp
turmeric, 1/4 tsp
vegetable broth, low sodium, 1 cup (or more as needed)

INSTRUCTIONS

1. In a large skillet over medium heat, saute ginger and onion in hot coconut oil for about 10 minutes until soft, translucent, and aromatic. Add garlic and saute for another minute.

2. In a small bowl, combine curry powder, cumin, coriander, garam masala, and turmeric. Stir into the skillet mixture. Continue stirring while adding vegetable broth slowly until the mixture reaches a consistency like paste.

3. Add the sweet potato, chickpeas, and 1 cup of vegetable broth. Reduce heat to simmering and cook for about 10 minutes until the sweet potato is tender.

4. Stir in the tomatoes and bring the mixture to a boil. Cook until the liquid is the consistency of a thick gravy.

CHICKPEA AND VEGETABLE SALAD SANDWICHES

Makes 2 servings

INGREDIENTS

Proteins:

chickpeas, canned (low sodium), 8 oz, rinsed and drained

Vegetables and Fruits:

onion, 1/2 small, minced
bell peppers, 1/2 small, minced finely
carrots, 1/2 small carrot, peeled and julienned
celery, 1/2 stalk, large, minced
cucumbers, 1/4 cup, shredded

Starch:

bread, whole grain rye, 2 slices

Fats:

olive oil, extra virgin, 2 tsp

Seasonings:

capers, 1-1/2 tsp
paprika, 1/4 tsp
chili powder, chipotle, 1/8 tsp
pepper, black, 1/8 tsp
Italian herb seasoning, salt free, dried, 1 tsp
vinegar, balsamic, 2 tsp

INSTRUCTIONS

1. Mix all ingredients except chickpeas and bread together in a large bowl and mix thoroughly. Gently fold in chickpeas.

2. Serve chickpea salad on whole grain bread or toast.

CHICKPEA SALAD WITH MINT AND BULGUR

Makes 2 servings

INGREDIENTS

Proteins:

chickpeas, canned (low sodium), 1 cup, drained and rinsed

Vegetables and Fruits:

tomatoes, 2 cups, diced
onion, 1/2 small, diced finely

Starch:

bulgur, 1/3 cup, dry, instant

Fats:

olive oil, extra virgin, 2 tsp
almonds, 2 tbsp, roughly chopped

Seasonings:

vegetable broth, low sodium, 3/4 cup
pepper, black, 1/2 tsp
orange zest, 1 tsp
mint, 2 tbsp, fresh, torn

INSTRUCTIONS

1. Bring vegetable broth to boil in a medium saucepan. Stir in the bulgur. Remove from heat and cover. Allow bulgur mixture to swell for 45 minutes.

2. Add almonds to a small saute pan over medium-high heat. Cook, stirring constantly to turn almond pieces, until golden brown. Remove almonds from pan.

3. Mix almonds, chickpeas, 1 tsp of olive oil, 1/4 tsp black pepper, and orange zest into the bulgur.

4. In a large bowl, combine tomatoes, onion, 1 tsp olive oil, mint, 1/4 tsp black pepper, and orange zest.

5. Serve the tomato mixture atop the bulgur and sprinkle with almonds.

CHICKPEAS AND EGG WHITES WITH SPINACH AND TOMATO

Makes 2 servings

INGREDIENTS

Proteins:

chickpeas, canned (low sodium), 1/2 cup, drained and rinsed
egg whites, 1/4 cup

Vegetables and Fruits:

shallots, 1 shallot, sliced thinly
tomato sauce, all natural, 1/4 cup
baby spinach, 1-1/2 cup, fresh

Starch:

bread, whole grain, 2 pieces

Fats:

olive oil, extra virgin, 2 tsp
pistachios, unsalted, shelled, 2 tbsp, chopped

Seasonings:

garlic, 1 clove, minced
rosemary, 1 tsp, fresh, chopped
pepper, black, 1/4 tsp
Italian herb seasoning, salt free, dried, 1 tsp

INSTRUCTIONS

1. Over medium heat, in a large skillet heat olive oil. Add shallot and cook for 2 minutes. Add garlic and cook another minute. Stir in rosemary and black pepper.

2. In a small bowl, combine tomato sauce and Italian seasoning. Add seasoned tomato sauce and chickpeas to skillet. Stir to combine and reduce heat to simmer.

3. Sprinkle mixture evenly with spinach and pistachios. Pour egg whites evenly over the mixture. Simmer, without stirring, until the egg whites are set, about 15 minutes.

4. Serve with toasted whole-grain bread.

COD AND POTATO CASSEROLE

Makes 2 servings

INGREDIENTS

Proteins:

cod, 8 oz

Vegetables and Fruits:

onion, 1 large, diced finely
tomatoes, 1 medium, diced
tomato sauce, all natural, 1/4 cup

Starch:

potatoes, skin on, 1 small potato, sliced thinly

Fats:

olive oil, extra virgin, 4 tsp

Seasonings:

garlic, 2 cloves, minced
pepper, crushed red, 1 tsp
paprika, 1 tsp
parsley, 1 tbsp, fresh, chopped

INSTRUCTIONS

1. Cut cod into small pieces and steam (or boil in water) for 5 minutes.

2. Preheat oven to 375 degrees F.

3. Add olive oil to a medium-hot saute pan, then add onion. Cook onion until tender and brown, about 8 minutes. Add garlic, crushed red pepper, and paprika and cook for another 45 seconds. Fold in the tomato and tomato sauce.

4. Line a small casserole dish with nonstick aluminum foil or parchment paper. Create a base layer with half of the potato slices, then layer the cod on top of it. Top with the remaining potato slices.

5. Pour the onion mixture over the dish so it covers everything evenly.

6. Bake for 45 minutes until the potato slices are tender. Garnish with parsley and serve.

COD MARINARA WITH LINGUINE

Makes 2 servings

INGREDIENTS

Proteins:

cod, 8 oz, fillet

Vegetables and Fruits:

onion, 1/2 small, chopped finely
tomato sauce, all natural, 1/2 cup
tomatoes, 1 cup, fresh, chopped

Starch:

pasta, whole grain, 2 oz dry weight, prepared according to package directions

Fats:

olive oil, extra virgin, 4 tsp

Seasonings:

garlic, 2 cloves, minced
pepper, black, 1/4 tsp
Italian herb seasoning, salt free, dried, 1 tsp
bay leaf, 1 leaf, chopped finely

INSTRUCTIONS

1. In a medium saucepan over medium heat, saute the onion in olive oil for about 5 minutes. Add the garlic and saute for 1 minute more. Stir in the tomato sauce, tomatoes, black pepper, bay leaf, and Italian herb seasoning.

2. Line a baking dish with nonstick foil or parchment paper. Pour half of the sauce into the pan. Place the fish on top, then cover with the remaining sauce.

3. Bake for 30 minutes or until the fish flakes easily with a fork.

4. Serve over prepared linguine.

CREAMY, LEMONY SHRIMP AND PASTA SALAD

Makes 2 servings

INGREDIENTS

Proteins:

yogurt, Greek, plain, nonfat, 2 tbsp
shrimp, 7 oz, thawed (if frozen), peeled, and deveined

Vegetables and Fruits:

lemons, 1 lemon, small, halved
broccoli, 1 cup, fresh, chopped, raw

Starch:

pasta, whole grain, 2/3 cup, dry, uncooked, penne

Fats:

olive oil, extra virgin, 4 tsp

Seasonings:

dijon mustard, 1-1/2 tsp
garlic, 4 cloves, minced
pepper, black, 1/2 tsp
scallions, 1/4 cups, chopped

INSTRUCTIONS

1. Mix Greek yogurt, juice from 1/2 lemon, dijon mustard, garlic, and 1/4 tsp black pepper together.

2. Cook penne in a large pot of boiling water for about 8-10 minutes, or until al dente. Drain. Rinse under cold water to cool. Toss with yogurt dressing.

3. Preheat oven to 450 degrees F.

4. Toss shrimp with olive oil and 1/4 tsp black pepper. Bake shrimp on a foil-lined baking sheet for 10-15 minutes until they are bright pink.

5. Slice remaining 1/2 lemon. Add shrimp, scallions, and raw broccoli to pasta salad and garnish with lemon slices.

CURRIED CHICKEN AND PLUM COUSCOUS STEW

Makes 2 servings

INGREDIENTS

Proteins:

chicken breast, boneless, skinless, 8 oz, cut into cubes

Vegetables and Fruits:

jalapeno peppers, 1 tbsp, diced
carrots, 1 small carrot, julienned
zucchini, 1/2 small zucchini, diced
plums, dried (prunes), 1/2 cup

Starch:

couscous, whole wheat, 1/4 cup, instant, dry

Fats:

olive oil, extra virgin, 4 tsp

Seasonings:

vegetable broth, low sodium, 1-3/4 cups
pepper, black, 1/4 tsp
scallions, 3 scallions, sliced thin
ginger, 3/4 tsp, fresh, peeled and grated
curry powder, 3/4 tsp
coriander seed, 1/4 tsp

INSTRUCTIONS

1. Bring 1 cup of vegetable broth to boil in a small saucepan. Stir in the couscous and dried plums. Remove from heat and cover. Allow couscous mixture to swell for 10 minutes.

2. Meanwhile, heat 2 tsp olive oil over medium heat in a medium skillet. Add chicken and black pepper. Cook, stirring, until juices run clear and chicken is no longer pink. Remove from skillet.

3. Heat the remaining 2 tsp oil in the skillet over medium heat. Add the jalapeno pepper and carrot and cook for about 2 minutes. Add the zucchini, scallions, ginger, curry powder, coriander seed, and remaining 3/4 cup of vegetable broth. Cook, stirring occasionally, until the vegetables are tender, or about 5 minutes.

4. Add the chicken to the skillet and heat through. Remove from heat, add couscous, and toss.

FISH CURRY, INDIAN-STYLE, WITH RICE AND SPINACH

Makes 2 servings

INGREDIENTS

Proteins:

cod, 8 oz, fillet

Vegetables and Fruits:

onion, 1/2 small, roughly chopped
tomatoes, 2 medium
spinach, 1 cup, shredded

Starch:

rice, whole grain brown or wild, 1/3 cup, dry measure, prepared with water according to package directions

Fats:

olive oil, extra virgin, 2 tsp
cashews, 2 tbsp

Seasonings:

dijon mustard, 2 tsp
ginger, 1/2 inch piece, fresh, peeled
garlic, 2 cloves, peeled
cumin, 3/4 tsp
turmeric, 3/4 tsp
pepper, cayenne, 1 tsp
vegetable broth, low sodium, 1/4 cup
cilantro, 2 tbsp, chopped, fresh

INSTRUCTIONS

1. Combine the dijon mustard and 1 tsp olive oil in a wide-mouthed bowl. Add the fish, then turn to coat both sides. Marinate for one hour.

2. Preheat oven to 350 degrees F.

3. Puree the cashews, ginger, onion, and garlic in a food processor or blender.

4. In a saute pan, heat the remaining 1 tsp olive oil over medium heat and add the puree. Cook, stirring constantly, for about a minute, then add the cumin, turmeric, and cayenne pepper and cook for another few minutes. Remove from heat. Stir in the vegetable broth, diced tomatoes, and spinach.

5. Place the fish in a foil-lined casserole dish and top with the vegetable mixture. Cover and bake for about half an hour until the fish is tender and flaky. Serve over a bed of cooked rice.

FISH STEW, MEDITERRANEAN STYLE, WITH PASTA

Makes 2 servings

INGREDIENTS

Proteins:

cod, 8 oz, fillet

Vegetables and Fruits:

onion, 2 small, diced finely
tomatoes, 2 medium, diced

Starch:

pasta, whole grain, 2 oz dry weight, rotini, bowtie, or similar

Fats:

olive oil, extra virgin, 4 tsp

Seasonings:

garlic, 2 cloves, minced
vegetable broth, low sodium, 3 cups
cinnamon, 1/2 tsp
cilantro, 1/2 cup, chopped, fresh
parsley, 1/2 cup, chopped, fresh
pepper, black, 1 tsp

INSTRUCTIONS

1. Heat the olive oil over medium heat in a large pot. Saute the onions until softened, stirring frequently, about 8 minutes, then add garlic and continue to saute for another minute.

2. Stir in the vegetable broth and bring to a boil.

3. Add the cod, tomatoes, cinnamon, cilantro, parsley, and black pepper. Reduce heat to simmering and cook for 10 minutes.

4. Add the pasta and continue simmering until the pasta is tender, about 6-10 minutes, depending on the type.

FISH TACOS

Makes 2 servings

INGREDIENTS

Proteins:

cod, 8 oz, fillet

Vegetables and Fruits:

watermelon, 1 cup, cut into small chunks, seeds removed
limes, 1 lime, juiced and zested
romaine lettuce hearts, 1 cup, shredded

Starch:

corn tortillas, whole grain, 4 tortillas

Fats:

avocado, 1/4 avocado, pitted, peeled, and sliced
olive oil, extra virgin, 2 tsp

Seasonings:

scallions, 1/4 cup, chopped
cilantro, 1/4 cup, fresh, chopped
chili powder, chipotle, 1/2 tsp

INSTRUCTIONS

1. Preheat a grill.

2. In a medium bowl, mix together the watermelon, scallions, cilantro, and the juice and zest from 1/2 of the lime.

3. Dust the fish on both sides with the chipotle chili powder.

4. Brush the grill with the olive oil. Grill the fish about 4-5 minutes per side until cooked through. Cod flake easily with a fork. Break the fish into small chunks.

5. Place the corn tortillas on the grill just long enough to warm them. Fill tortillas with fish, avocado, lettuce, and the watermelon mixture.

6. Cut the remaining 1/2 lime into wedges and serve alongside the tacos.

GAZPACHO SALAD

Makes 2 servings

INGREDIENTS

Proteins:

cod, 8 oz, fillet

Vegetables and Fruits:

tomatoes, 1 large, diced
onion, 2 small, diced

Starch:

cereal, whole grain, shredded wheat style, spoon size, unsweetened, 1 cup

Fats:

avocado, 1/4 avocado, peeled and diced
olive oil, extra virgin, 2 tsp

Seasonings:

vinegar, white balsamic, 1/2 tsp
pepper, black, 1/4 tsp

INSTRUCTIONS

1. In a medium bowl, combine tomato, onion, and avocado. Drizzle with olive oil and vinegar. Season with pepper.

2. Refrigerate for one hour.

3. Steam or boil cod for 10 minutes until cooked through. Let cool.

4. Place cod on salad and crumble shredded wheat cereal on top.

GINGER-CARROT TOFU SOUP

Makes 2 servings

INGREDIENTS

Proteins:

tofu, 6 oz, extra-firm, squeezed between paper towels and cut into 1" cubes

Vegetables and Fruits:

onion, 1 small, diced
carrots, 2-1/4 cups, frozen, defrosted and roughly chopped

Starch:

oats, rolled, 1/2 cup, uncooked

Fats:

coconut oil, 4 tsp

Seasonings:

ginger, 1 piece, 1-1/2", grated
pepper, black, 1/4 tsp
Chinese five-spice powder, 1/4 tsp
vegetable broth, low sodium, 3 cups
curry powder, 3/4 tsp

INSTRUCTIONS

1. Over medium heat in a large saucepan, heat 1 tsp coconut oil. Add the onions, carrots, ginger, and black pepper and cook for 8 minutes, stirring frequently.

2. Add the Chinese five-spice powder and vegetable broth. Bring to a boil, then reduce to a simmer, cover, and cook for 20 minutes or until the vegetables are tender.

3. In a food processor or blender, pulse the rolled oats into flour. Combine the curry powder and oat flour on a plate. Press the tofu chunks into the seasoned oat flour on all sides.

4. In a large skillet, heat the remaining 3 tsp coconut oil over medium-high heat. Add the tofu in batches, turning to crisp on all sides, approximately 5 minutes total.

5. Puree the soup with a food processor or blender. Pour into bowls and serve with fried tofu.

GRILLED CHICKEN BREASTS WITH CORN APPLE RELISH

Makes 2 servings

INGREDIENTS

Proteins:

chicken breast, boneless, skinless, 8 oz

Vegetables and Fruits:

apples, 1 small, diced
onion, 2 tbsp, diced
limes, 2 tbsp, juice only

Starch:

corn, 1 cup, frozen kernels, defrosted

Fats:

olive oil, extra virgin, 4 tsp

Seasonings:

chili powder, chipotle, 1/2 tsp
cumin, 1/4 tsp
pepper, crushed red, 1/8 tsp
pepper, black, 1/2 tsp
parsley, 1 tbsp, fresh, minced

INSTRUCTIONS

1. Preheat a grill or grill pan to medium-high heat.

2. In a small bowl, combine chili powder, cumin, crushed red pepper, and 1/4 tsp black pepper.

3. Brush both sides of chicken breasts with 2 tsp olive oil and sprinkle on the spice mixture. Grill approximately 10 minutes, turning once, or until cooked through.

4. In a medium bowl, mix corn, apples, onions, parsley, lime juice, remaining 2 tsp olive oil, and 1/4 tsp black pepper. Top chicken with relish and serve.

GRILLED CUMIN CHICKEN BREASTS WITH SWEET POTATO COLESLAW

Makes 2 servings

INGREDIENTS

Proteins:

chicken breast, boneless, skinless, 8 oz

Vegetables and Fruits:

apples, 1 small, peeled, cored, and julienned
cabbage, 3/4 cup, shredded
carrots, 1/4 cup, peeled and julienned

Starch:

sweet potatoes, 2/3 cup, raw, peeled and finely julienned

Fats:

olive oil, extra virgin, 4 tsp

Seasonings:

vinegar, cider, 1 tbsp
pepper, black, 1/2 tsp
scallions, 1 tbsp, sliced thin
cumin, 1/2 tsp

INSTRUCTIONS

1. In a small bowl, make the coleslaw dressing by combining 3 tsp of olive oil with the cider vinegar and 1/4 tsp pepper.

2. In a medium bowl, toss together apple, cabbage, carrot, sweet potato, and scallions.

3. Preheat a grill or grill pan to medium-high.

4. Brush chicken breast with 1 tsp olive oil. Mix together cumin and 1/4 tsp pepper and rub onto chicken breast.

5. Grill breast for 4-5 minutes per side, or until the chicken is cooked through and no longer pink inside. Let rest for 5 minutes.

6. Drizzle the dressing over the coleslaw and toss to mix well.

GRILLED GROUPER WITH MANGO SALSA AND MIXED GREENS

Makes 2 servings

INGREDIENTS

Proteins:

grouper, 8 oz, fillet

Vegetables and Fruits:

bell peppers, 1 pepper, small, red
mango, 1/4 cup, cubed
pineapples, 1/4 cup, cubed
papaya, 1/4 cup, cubed
jalapeno peppers, 1/4 pepper, seeded and minced finely
baby mixed greens, 1 cup
limes, 1 lime, juiced

Starch:

corn, 1 cup kernels, roasted or boiled

Fats:

olive oil, extra virgin, 4 tsp

Seasonings:

cajun seasoning, 1 tsp, or to taste
cilantro, 1/4 cup, chopped

INSTRUCTIONS

1. Roast the red pepper on the grill or 6" from a broiler element until the skin is blackened all around, turning frequently. Let cool, then remove skin and dice.

2. In a medium bowl, combine diced peppers, corn, mangos, pineapple, papaya, and minced jalapeno with lime juice to create a salsa.

3. Sprinkle both sides of the grouper with cajun spice.

4. Heat olive oil in a cast iron frying pan until it begins to smoke. Add the grouper and cook 3 minutes on each side or until cooked through.

5. Serve grouper on top of mixed greens, then spoon salsa on top. Garnish with cilantro.

GRILLED SALMON WITH CUCUMBER DILL SALAD

Makes 2 servings

INGREDIENTS

Proteins:

yogurt, Greek, plain, nonfat, 3 tbsp
salmon, 7 oz

Vegetables and Fruits:

cucumbers, 1/2 lb, sliced thinly
onion, 1/4 medium, sliced thinly

Starch:

rye crisps, whole grain, 4 crisps

Fats:

olive oil, extra virgin, 4 tsp

Seasonings:

dill, 1/2 tsp, dried
vinegar, red wine, 1 tbsp
pepper, black, 1/2 tsp

INSTRUCTIONS

1. Preheat grill or grill plate.

2. Use paper towels to dry the cucumber slices. Combine in a medium bowl with yogurt, onion, dill, 2 tsp of the olive oil, vinegar, and 1/4 tsp pepper.

3. Brush both sides of the salmon with the remaining 2 tsp olive oil and season with the remaining 1/4 tsp pepper.

4. Grill the salmon for about 3 minutes on each side, only long enough for it to become opaque.

5. Serve with the cucumber salad and rye crisps.

GRILLED SHRIMP WITH SOBA NOODLES

Makes 2 servings

INGREDIENTS

Proteins:

shrimp, 8 oz, defrosted (if frozen), shelled and deveined

Vegetables and Fruits:

shallots, 1 large, sliced thinly and divided into rings
limes, 2 limes
apples, 2 small, diced finely

Starch:

soba noodles, whole grain, 1-1/2 oz, uncooked

Fats:

olive oil, extra virgin, 4 tsp

Seasonings:

garlic, 2 cloves, minced
pepper, crushed red, 1/4 tsp
pepper, black, 1/4 tsp
cilantro, 2 tbsp, fresh, chopped

INSTRUCTIONS

1. Heat 2 tsp olive oil in a small skillet over medium heat. Add shallots and cook for 2 minutes. Add the garlic and continue stirring until the shallots are crisp and golden, about 1-2 minutes. Let cool.

2. Add noodles to a large pot of boiling water and cook, stirring, about 4 minutes, or until tender. Drain in a colander and rinse thoroughly under cold, running water. Transfer to a large bowl and toss with the shallot-garlic mixture.

3. Zest and juice one of the limes. Preheat a grill or grill pan on medium-high. Toss shrimp in a medium-sized bowl with 1 tsp lime zest, 2 tbsp lime juice, 2 tsp olive oil, and the crushed and black peppers.

4. Grill shrimp, turning once, until they just turn opaque throughout, about 3 minutes.

5. Arrange noodles on plates. Top with cilantro and shrimp. Serve with the second lime, cut into wedges.

HALIBUT AND CAPONATA PITA

Makes 2 servings

INGREDIENTS

Proteins:

halibut, 8 oz, fillet

Vegetables and Fruits:

onion, 1 red, small, diced
artichokes, 1/2 cup hearts, frozen, diced
celery, 1 stalk, chopped
tomatoes, 1 large, diced
raisins, 1/4 cup

Starch:

pita, whole grain, 1 pita, separated into halves

Fats:

olive oil, extra virgin, 4 tsp

Seasonings:

pepper, black, 1/2 tsp
vinegar, red wine, 2 tbsp
capers, 1/2 tbsp, rinsed and drained
parsley, 4 sprigs

INSTRUCTIONS

1. First, make the caponata. Heat the olive oil in a large skillet over medium heat. Add the onion and 1/4 tsp black pepper. Cook for 3 minutes until the onion begins to soften. Add the artichoke hearts and celery. Continue cooking, stirring occasionally, until the artichokes become lightly browned, about 4 minutes.

2. Stir in the tomatoes and raisins. Reduce heat and simmer for 20-30 minutes until the mixture thickens, occasionally stirring. Add the vinegar and capers.

3. Next, prepare the halibut. Preheat oven to 400 degrees F and line a baking sheet with nonstick foil or parchment paper. Sprinkle the halibut with 1/4 tsp black pepper, place on the baking sheet, and roast for 10-12 minutes, or until it flakes easily with a fork.

4. Flake the halibut with a fork into the pita pockets and then add the caponata and finally fresh parsley.

HALIBUT VERACRUZ

Makes 2 servings

INGREDIENTS

Proteins:

    halibut, 8 oz, fillet

Vegetables and Fruits:

    onion, 1 small, diced
    tomatoes, 1 medium, diced
    baby spinach, 1 cup, shredded
    jalapeno peppers, 1/4 seeded and finely diced
    limes, 1 lime, juiced

Starch:

    rice, whole grain brown or wild, 1/3 cup dry measure, prepared with water according to package directions

Fats:

    olive oil, extra virgin, 2 tsp
    avocado, 1/4 peeled and sliced

Seasonings:

    garlic, 2 cloves, minced
    vegetable broth, low sodium, 1/4 cups
    cilantro, 1 tbsp, chopped

INSTRUCTIONS

1. Preheat oven to 350 degrees F.

2. Heat olive oil over medium heat. Saute onion for 3 minutes, then add garlic and continue cooking for 1 minute.

3. Add the tomatoes, shredded spinach, jalapeno, and vegetable broth. Cook to reduce the juices down by 2/3.

4. Place the fish in the prepared baking pan and cook for 10 minutes.

5. To serve, layer the prepared rice on the plate, then the sauce, then the halibut, then the sliced avocado, and finally the cilantro. Squeeze lime juice atop.

HEARTY ITALIAN WEDDING SOUP

Makes 2 servings

INGREDIENTS

Proteins:

turkey, ground, extra lean, 8 oz

Vegetables and Fruits:

endive, 2 cups, finely sliced

Starch:

barley, 1/4 cup, whole grain, raw, uncooked

Fats:

pistachios, unsalted, shelled, 1/4 cup

Seasonings:

basil, 1 tbsp, fresh, chopped
parsley, 2 tbsp, fresh, chopped
scallions, 2 scallions, sliced thinly
vegetable broth, low sodium, 3 cups
lemon zest, 2 tbsp

INSTRUCTIONS

1. Grind pistachios in spice grinder, in small food processor, or with a mortar and pestle.

2. Mix turkey, ground pistachios, basil, parsley, and scallions. Shape into tight 3/4" balls.

3. Bring vegetable broth to boiling. Drop in meatballs. Stir in the endive, barley, and lemon zest. Reduce heat to medium.

4. Continue to cook until barley is tender, stirring frequently, about 15 minutes.

HERB-CRUSTED HALIBUT WITH SAUTEED BOK CHOY

Makes 2 servings

INGREDIENTS

Proteins:

halibut, 8 oz, fillet

Vegetables and Fruits:

bok choy, 6 oz, leaves only, shredded or chopped into bite-sized pieces

Starch:

bread, whole grain, 2 slices

Fats:

olive oil, extra virgin, 4 tsp

Seasonings:

parsley, 2 tbsp, fresh, chopped
dill, 2 tbsp, fresh, chopped
lemon zest, 1 tsp
pepper, black, 1/2 tsp
garlic, 1 clove, minced

INSTRUCTIONS

1. Place bread slices on oven rack and cook at 250 degrees F until very dry, about an hour. Remove from oven and pulse in food processor or blender, or chop with a knife, to create large crumbs.

2. Preheat oven to 400 degrees F. Line a baking sheet with nonstick aluminum foil.

3. In a medium bowl, toss bread crumbs with chopped parsley, dill, lemon zest, 1/4 tsp black pepper, and 2 tsp olive oil.

4. Place the halibut on the prepared baking tray. Top with the herbed bread crumbs, pressing lightly so that it adheres to the fish.

5. Bake for 10-15 minutes until the fish flakes easily with a fork and crumbs become lightly browned.

6. While the fish bakes, prepare the bok choy. In a saucepan over medium heat, heat the remaining 2 tsp of olive oil, then add the garlic and cook for 1-2 minutes. Add the shredded or chopped bok choy and continue to cook for 5 minutes until the leaves become bright green.

ITALIAN-STYLE TURKEY MEATBALLS AND SPAGHETTI

Makes 2 servings

INGREDIENTS

Proteins:

turkey, ground, extra lean, 8 oz

Vegetables and Fruits:

onion, 1 small, diced
tomatoes, 2 small, diced
tomato sauce, all natural, 1 cup

Starch:

pasta, whole grain, 2 oz, spaghetti, dry

Fats:

olive oil, extra virgin, 4 tsp

Seasonings:

garlic, 3 cloves, minced
parsley, 2 tbsp, fresh, chopped
oregano, 1 tbsp, fresh, chopped
rosemary, 1 tsp, fresh, chopped
dijon mustard, 1 tsp
Italian herb seasoning, salt free, dried, 1 tbsp

INSTRUCTIONS

1. In a small saucepan, heat 2 tsp olive oil over medium heat. Add onion and cook, stirring often, until it begins to soften and become translucent, about 8 minutes. Add garlic and cook for another minute.

2. Add tomatoes, tomato sauce, parsley, oregano, rosemary and dijon mustard and stir. Bring to a boil, then reduce to a simmer.

3. Mix ground turkey with Italian seasoning mix. Roll into 10 small balls.

4. Heat 2 tsp olive oil in a medium skillet over medium heat.

5. Fry the meatballs, turning occasionally, until brown on all sides. Add the meatballs to the sauce and continue simmering until the insides are done, about 10 minutes. Test for doneness by cutting a meatball and checking to make sure there is no pink at the center.

6. Cook the spaghetti in boiling water in a medium-sized stockpot until crisp-tender, about 10 minutes. Drain and serve with meatballs and sauce.

LEMON GRILLED COD WITH ASPARAGUS AND WILD RICE

Makes 2 servings

INGREDIENTS

Proteins:

cod, 8 oz, fillet, cut into 2 equal portions

Vegetables and Fruits:

lemons, 1 lemon, juiced
asparagus, 10 medium

Starch:

rice, whole grain brown or wild, 1/3 cup, dry measure, prepared with water according to package directions

Fats:

olive oil, extra virgin, 4 tsp

Seasonings:

cajun seasoning, 1 tsp
pepper, black, 1/4 tsp
pepper, lemon, 1/2 tsp
scallions, 1 tbsp, chopped

INSTRUCTIONS

1. Mix the cajun seasoning, black pepper, lemon pepper, and olive oil together. Brush onto both sides of the cod and allow to marinate for one hour.

2. Preheat grill or grill pan.

3. Trim off the woody ends of the asparagus. Wrap in a single layer in aluminum foil. Seal the edges and place on the grill for 9 minutes.

4. Meanwhile, in a small saucepan, combine lemon juice and scallions over medium heat and stir for three minutes or until the scallions soften.

5. After the asparagus has cooked for 9 minutes, add the cod to the grill, allowing the asparagus to continue cooking. Grill the cod until brown and flaky, about three minutes per side.

6. Serve the cod and asparagus over the prepared rice. Drizzle with the lemon juice and scallion mixture.

MARINATED SALMON WITH BROCCOLI AND RICE

Makes 2 servings

INGREDIENTS

Proteins:

salmon, 8 oz, fillet

Vegetables and Fruits:

lemons, 1 small, juiced
broccoli, 2 cups florets, fresh

Starch:

rice, whole grain brown or wild, 1/3 cup, raw, uncooked

Fats:

olive oil, extra virgin, 4 tsp

Seasonings:

pepper, black, 1/4 tsp
pepper, crushed red, 1/2 tsp
vinegar, balsamic, 2 tsp
garlic, 2 cloves, minced
scallions, 2 tbsp, chopped finely
cilantro, 1 tbsp, chopped
water, 1 cup

INSTRUCTIONS

1. Season salmon with black pepper and crushed red pepper. Slice each broccoli floret lengthwise, halving it.

2. Mix 4 tsp of the lemon juice with 2 tsp olive oil, balsamic vinegar, garlic, scallions, and cilantro in a medium bowl or plastic bag. Add salmon and broccoli and toss to coat. Cover bowl or seal bag and refrigerate at least 5 hours.

3. Drain marinade into a large, microwave-safe bowl. Add water and rice and stir. Microwave on 70% power for about 20 minutes (microwaves vary), or until all liquid is absorbed and rice is tender. Let rice rest.

4. Preheat broiler. Brush with remaining 2 tsp olive oil. Place salmon and broccoli on a broiler tray and cook for about 5 minutes on each side, until the salmon becomes opaque and the broccoli is tender and browned.

5. Fluff rice with a fork. Serve salmon and broccoli over rice with remaining lemon juice.

MEDITERRANEAN CHICKPEA SOUP

Makes 2 servings

INGREDIENTS

Proteins:

chickpeas, canned (low sodium), 1 cup, drained and rinsed

Vegetables and Fruits:

onion, 1 small, diced finely
tomatoes, 2 small, diced finely

Starch:

pita, whole grain, 1 pita, halved

Fats:

olive oil, extra virgin, 4 tsp

Seasonings:

garlic, 3 cloves, minced
rosemary, 1/2 tsp, fresh, minced
pepper, black, 1/4 tsp
vegetable broth, low sodium, 2 cups
vinegar, balsamic, 1-1/2 tsp

INSTRUCTIONS

1. Over medium heat in a large saucepan, heat olive oil. Add onion and cook, stirring frequently, until tender and translucent, about 8 minutes. Add garlic and stir for one minute more.

2. Add the chickpeas, tomatoes, rosemary, black pepper, and vegetable broth. Bring to a boil, then reduce heat to simmering. Cook for 20 minutes.

3. Allow the soup to cool to room temperature. Puree half the soup in a blender or food processor, then return to saucepan.

4. Add the vinegar, stirring to combine, then bring to a boil.

5. Serve with pita halves.

MEDITERRANEAN-STYLE MAHI MAHI AND BARLEY SALAD

Makes 2 servings

INGREDIENTS

Proteins:

mahi mahi, 8 oz fillet

Vegetables and Fruits:

lemons, 2 lemons, juiced and zested
baby spinach, 1-1/2 cups
tomatoes, 1/2 cup, diced

Starch:

barley, 1/4 cup, whole grain, raw, uncooked

Fats:

olive oil, extra virgin, 4 tsp

Seasonings:

oregano, 1-1/2 tbsp
spearmint, 1-1/2 tbsp
garlic, 1 clove, minced
vegetable broth, low sodium, 1 cup

INSTRUCTIONS

1. In a resealable plastic bag or shallow bowl, combine lemon juice, 3 tsp olive oil, oregano, spearmint, 1/2 tsp lemon zest, and garlic. Shake to combine.

2. Add fish and marinate for 1 hour, turning once. Meanwhile, make the barley by bringing it to a boil in the vegetable broth, then reduce to simmer for 45 minutes, or until tender. Drain and let cool.

3. Remove fish from marinade and in a small saucepan bring marinade to a boil. Place in the refrigerator to cool.

4. Heat nonstick grill or grill plate to medium. Brush with remaining 1 tsp olive oil.

5. Cook fish, turning once, until it flakes easily with a fork, 10-13 minutes.

6. While the fish cooks, assemble the salad by combining the tomatoes and spinach with the cooked and cooled barley. Toss with the marinade and serve.

OVEN-FRIED CHICKEN BREASTS AND VEGETABLES

Makes 2 servings

INGREDIENTS

Proteins:

yogurt, Greek, plain, nonfat, 3 oz
chicken breast, boneless, skinless, 6 oz

Vegetables and Fruits:

green beans, 2 cups, fresh

Starch:

rye crisps, whole grain, 4 crisps

Fats:

olive oil, extra virgin, 1 tsp
almonds, 3 tbsp

Seasonings:

pepper, black, 1/2 tsp
paprika, 1/4 tsp
dijon mustard, 1/4 tsp
scallions, 1 tbsp, sliced thinly
lemon zest, 1/4 tsp

INSTRUCTIONS

1. Preheat oven to 450 degrees F. Place a cooking rack onto a baking sheet lined with aluminum foil. Brush the rack with the olive oil.

2. Grind the rye crisps and almonds in a food processor or spice grinder, or use a mortar and pestle. Transfer to a shallow bowl and mix in 1/4 tsp black pepper and paprika.

3. Mix mustard and yogurt together in a second shallow bowl. Dip one side of the chicken breasts in yogurt, then sprinkle crumb topping on. Dip the second side in yogurt and crumbs.

4. Place coated chicken onto the prepared rack and top with scallions. Insert a thermometer into the thickest section of breasts. Bake until the thermometer reads 160 degrees F, about 30 minutes. Remove from the oven and allow to rest for at least 5 minutes.

5. Add green beans to boiling water. Cook for 5-10 minutes until beans are crisp-tender.

6. Toss beans with lemon zest and 1/4 tsp black pepper before serving.

POACHED SALMON WITH ALMOND COUSCOUS

Makes 2 servings

INGREDIENTS

Proteins:

salmon, 8 oz, fillet

Vegetables and Fruits:

baby spinach, 2 cups, chopped
celery, 1/4 cup, chopped
tomatoes, 1/2 tomato, diced

Starch:

couscous, whole wheat, 1/4 cup, dry, uncooked

Fats:

almonds, 4 tbsp

Seasonings:

vegetable broth, low sodium, 2-1/2 cups
parsley, 1 tsp, dried
pepper, crushed red, 1 tsp
savory, 1 tsp
lemon zest, 1 tbsp
scallions, 1 tbsp, chopped finely
pepper, black, 1/4 tsp
dill, 1 bunch, tied with twine

INSTRUCTIONS

1. First, prepare the couscous. In a small saucepan, bring 1/2 cup of vegetable broth to a boil. Add the parsley, crushed red pepper, and savory. Add the couscous, stirring to combine. Simmer until the couscous is tender, about ten minutes. Stir in the spinach. Allow to cool, then drain any excess liquid that remains.

2. In a salad bowl, combine the couscous with the lemon zest, almonds, celery, scallions, and tomato. Season with black pepper. Refrigerate at least one hour.

3. Next, prepare the salmon. In a medium saucepan, combine remaining 2 cups of vegetable broth, salmon, and dill. Bring to a boil, then reduce to a simmer. Cover the pot. Continue cooking until the fish flakes easily with a fork, about 15 minutes.

4. Serve salmon with salad.

ROASTED SALMON WITH LEEKS AND FINGERLING POTATOES

Makes 2 servings

INGREDIENTS

Proteins:

salmon, 8 oz, fillet

Vegetables and Fruits:

leeks, 3 leeks
shallots, 1 shallot
lemons, 1 lemon, juiced

Starch:

potatoes, skin on, 5 oz, fingerling

Fats:

olive oil, extra virgin, 4 tsp

Seasonings:

black pepper, 1/4 tsp
chives, 2 tsp, chopped
tarragon, 1 tsp, fresh
parsley, 1 tsp, fresh

INSTRUCTIONS

1. Preheat oven to 450 degrees F and cover a roasting pan or tray with parchment paper.

2. Clean the leeks thoroughly, trimming away the green. Cut each leek lengthwise into quarters. Toss with 2 tsp olive oil and spread out on roasting pan. Roast for about 30 minutes, or until just golden.

3. Reduce heat to 275 degrees F. Use a brush to rub both sides of the salmon with the residual oil in the leek pan and season fish with black pepper. Place the salmon on top of the leeks and roast for about 30-40 minutes until the salmon is firm.

4. Meanwhile, boil the potatoes about 10 minutes, or until tender.

5. Mix the shallot, chives, tarragon, parsley, lemon juice, and remaining 2 tsp of olive oil in a food processor.

6. Serve the salmon, potatoes, and leeks with the shallot-herb mixture.

ROSEMARY DIJON CHICKEN BREASTS WITH CORN AND BRUSSELS SPROUTS

Makes 2 servings

INGREDIENTS

Proteins:

chicken breast, boneless, skinless, 8 oz

Vegetables and Fruits:

lemons, 1 lemon, juice only
brussels sprouts, 8 medium sprouts, cut in half

Starch:

corn, 2/3 cups, frozen, kernels

Fats:

olive oil, extra virgin, 4 tsp

Seasonings:

rosemary, 1 tbsp, fresh, minced
dijon mustard, 1 tbsp
pepper, black, 1/2 tsp
garlic, 4 cloves, minced

INSTRUCTIONS

1. In a large, shallow bowl or resealable plastic bag, combine 1 tbsp lemon juice, 2 tsp olive oil, rosemary, dijon mustard, pepper, and garlic. Add chicken, making sure to coat throughly. Let marinate in refrigerator for at least 30 minutes.

2. Preheat oven to 400 degrees F. Line a large baking sheet with aluminum foil. Brush brussels sprouts with 2 tsp of olive oil, dust with 1/4 tsp black pepper, and place on baking sheet.

3. Add the chicken to the baking sheet. Insert a thermometer into the thickest section of breast. Bake until the thermometer reads 160 degrees F, about 30 minutes.

4. Remove tray from the oven and allow to rest.

5. Add corn to a small pot of boiling water and cook until just tender, about 4-5 minutes. Drizzle remaining lemon juice over corn and brussels sprouts and serve with chicken.

SAFFRON TURKEY MEATBALLS IN BROTH

Makes 2 servings

INGREDIENTS

Proteins:

turkey, ground, extra lean, 8 oz

Vegetables and Fruits:

onion, 1 small, diced
celery, 2 stalks, sliced into 1" pieces

Starch:

rye flakes, whole grain, 1/4 cup

Fats:

pistachios, unsalted, shelled, 1 tbsp, chopped coarsely
olive oil, extra virgin, 2 tsp

Seasonings:

garlic, 1 clove
vegetable broth, low sodium, 2 cups
saffron, 1/8 tsp, powdered
parsley, 1/2 cup, fresh, leaves, minced

INSTRUCTIONS

1. Preheat oven to 350 degrees F. Toast rye flakes on a baking sheet for 5 minutes or until slightly browned.

2. Combine turkey with onion, garlic, toasted rye flakes, and pistachios. Shape into 10 small meatballs.

3. Over medium heat in a medium saucepan, heat olive oil. Add meatballs and cook for about 4 minutes per side or until browned, turning as needed.

4. Add the vegetable broth, saffron, and celery pieces. Bring to a boil, then reduce to simmer. Continue cooking for 10 minutes, or until meatballs are no longer pink in the center.

5. Serve broth in a shallow bowl. Top with meatballs and garnish with parsley.

SALMON AND LENTIL SALAD

Makes 2 servings

INGREDIENTS

Proteins:

salmon, 4 oz, fillet
lentils, 3 tbsp, dry (uncooked)

Vegetables and Fruits:

onion, 1 small, red, diced
cucumbers, 1 large, diced

Starch:

rye crisps, whole grain, 4 crisps

Fats:

olive oil, extra virgin, 4 tsp

Seasonings:

vegetable broth, low sodium, 1/2 cup
vinegar, balsamic, 4 tsp
garlic, 1 clove, minced
pepper, black, 1/4 tsp
pepper, lemon, 1/4 tsp

INSTRUCTIONS

1. In a small pot, cook lentils in vegetable broth for 10-15 minutes until tender. Allow to cool.

2. Preheat broiler and brush rack with 1 tsp olive oil. Place salmon on rack 6" below heating element. Broil for approximately 5 minutes per side, or until the salmon flakes easily.

3. All the salmon to cool, then chop or flake it into a medium bowl. Add the cooked lentils, red onion, and cucumber.

4. In a small bowl, whisk together the remaining 3 tsp olive oil, balsamic vinegar, garlic, black pepper, and lemon pepper. Drizzle over the salad and gently stir to coat.

5. Serve with rye crisps.

SALMON HASH WITH ARUGULA

Makes 2 servings

INGREDIENTS

Proteins:

> **salmon**, 6 oz, fillet, cut into bite-sized pieces
> **yogurt, Greek**, plain, nonfat, 2 tbsp

Vegetables and Fruits:

> **onion**, 1/2 small, sliced thinly
> **bell peppers**, 1 chopped, any color
> **arugula**, 1-1/2 cups, baby
> **lemons**, 1/2 lemon, cut into wedges

Starch:

> **potatoes, skin on**, 5 oz, shredded

Fats:

> **olive oil, extra virgin**, 4 tsp

Seasonings:

> **dijon mustard**, 1/2 tsp
> **dill**, 1 tbsp, fresh, chopped
> **pepper, black**, 1/4 tsp

INSTRUCTIONS

1. In a small bowl, combine the yogurt, mustard, and dill.

2. To a saucepan over medium heat, add 2 tsp olive oil, the shredded potatoes, and black pepper. Cook, stirring periodically, for 6 minutes.

3. Add the remaining oil, onion, and bell peppers and cook for 8 more minutes.

4. Add the salmon and cook for about 3 more minutes, just until the fish is cooked through.

5. Remove the pan from the heat. Stir in half of the yogurt mixture. Add a tsp of water to the remaining yogurt and toss with the arugula.

6. Serve with lemon wedges.

SHREDDED CHICKEN QUINOA PILAF

Makes 2 servings

INGREDIENTS

Proteins:

chicken breast, boneless, skinless, 8 oz

Vegetables and Fruits:

onion, 1 small, diced
celery, 1 stalk, diced
carrots, 3 small carrots, peeled and julienned
bok choy, 1 cup, fresh, leaves only, shredded

Starch:

quinoa, 2/3 cup, dry, uncooked

Fats:

coconut oil, 4 tsp

Seasonings:

vegetable broth, low sodium, 2 cups
Italian herb seasoning, salt free, dried, 1 tbsp
sage, 1 tsp, fresh, chopped
pepper, black, 1/4 tsp

INSTRUCTIONS

1. Dice chicken breasts into 1" cubes. Bring a medium saucepan filled with water to a boil. Add chicken breast pieces and allow water to return to a boil. Turn water off.

2. Leave the chicken in the hot water until cooked through, about 10 minutes. Test for doneness by poking the largest piece with a fork. If the juices run clear, the chicken is done.

3. Drain the chicken and set aside.

4. Heat the coconut oil over medium heat in the medium saucepan. Add the bok choy, onion, celery, and carrots and cook until tender, about 7-8 minutes.

5. Add the quinoa, vegetable broth, Italian herb seasoning, sage, and pepper. Bring to a boil, then reduce heat to simmering. Cover and cook until the quinoa has absorbed the liquid and become tender, approximately 20 minutes. Add the chicken and heat through.

SHRIMP SKEWERS WITH ORANGE-PLUM COUSCOUS

Makes 2 servings

INGREDIENTS

Proteins:

shrimp, 5 oz, thawed (if frozen), peeled, and deveined
yogurt, nonfat (0%) vanilla, 1/4 cup

Vegetables and Fruits:

plums, dried (prunes), 1/2 cup, chopped
oranges, 1 small orange

Starch:

couscous, whole wheat, 1/4 cups, instant, dry

Fats:

coconut oil, 4 tsp

Seasonings:

water, 1/4 cup
vinegar, balsamic, 2 tbsp
rosemary, 1/2 tsp, dried, crushed
vegetable broth, low sodium, 1 cup
scallions, 2 tbsp, sliced

INSTRUCTIONS

1. In a large bowl, combine the vanilla yogurt, water, balsamic vinegar, 3 tsp coconut oil, and rosemary. Add shrimp, coating thoroughly. Allow to marinate for at least 30 minutes in the refrigerator.

2. Bring vegetable broth to boil in a small saucepan. Stir in the couscous and dried plums. Remove from heat and cover. Allow couscous mixture to swell for 10 minutes.

3. Finely shred 1/2 tsp of orange peel. Juice the orange. Add orange peel, orange juice, and scallions to the couscous.

4. Preheat a grill or grill plate at medium heat. Brush with remaining 1 tsp coconut oil. Thread the shrimp onto skewers, leaving small gaps between them. Place on grill rack and cook until the shrimp are opaque, about 4 minutes per side, turning once.

5. Top couscous with shrimp.

SLOW COOKER CHICKEN TIKKA MASALA

Makes 2 servings

INGREDIENTS

Proteins:

chicken breast, boneless, skinless, 6 oz
yogurt, Greek, plain, nonfat, 1/2 cup

Vegetables and Fruits:

jalapeno peppers, 1 small, seeds removed, minced finely
tomato sauce, all natural, 1 cup
lemons, 1 lemon, cut into 8 wedges

Starch:

rice, whole grain brown or wild, 1/3 cup, dry measure, prepared with water
according to package directions

Fats:

peanuts, 4 tbsp, chopped

Seasonings:

ginger, 1 tbsp, fresh, minced
cumin, 1-1/ tsp
garam masala, 1 tsp
pepper, black, 1/4 tsp
paprika, 1 tsp
garlic, 4 cloves
cinnamon, 1/2 tsp
coriander seed, 1/2 tsp

INSTRUCTIONS

1. In a slow cooker, combine chicken, yogurt, jalapeno pepper, tomato sauce, ginger, cumin, garam masala, black pepper, paprika, garlic, cinnamon, and coriander in a slow cooker.

2. Cook on low for 6-8 hours until chicken is cooked through and very tender. Spoon over prepared rice. Sprinkle peanuts on top and serve with lemon wedges.

STIR-FRIED CHICKEN WITH CABBAGE, CHILE PASTE, AND SOBA NOODLES

Makes 2 servings

INGREDIENTS

Proteins:

chicken breast, boneless, skinless, 8 oz, cut into bite-sized pieces.

Vegetables and Fruits:

shallots, 1 shallot, peeled and roughly chopped
jalapeno peppers, 1/2 small, seeds removed
limes, 1 small lime
carrots, 1 small, peeled and cut into matchsticks
onion, 1 small, peeled and sliced
bok choy, 1 cup, leaves only, shredded

Starch:

soba noodles, whole grain, 1.5 oz, uncooked

Fats:

olive oil, extra virgin, 4 tsp

Seasonings:

garlic, 4 cloves
lemongrass, 1 stalk, white part only, roughly chopped
ginger, 1 piece, 1-1/2", peeled

INSTRUCTIONS

1. Make chili paste. Combine in a food processor the shallot, jalapeno pepper, garlic, lemongrass, and ginger. Squeeze just enough lime juice in to create a paste-like consistency.

2. Cook soba noodles in boiling water for about 4 minutes, stirring frequently, until tender. Drain in colander and rinse well under cold, running water. Transfer to a bowl and toss with 1 tsp olive oil.

3. Over medium high heat in a large pot, heat olive oil. Saute chicken for 1 minute, stirring frequently, then add chili paste, onions, bok choy, and carrots. Cook, stirring occasionally, until bok choy is wilted, about 4 minutes. Add the noodles and cook until the chicken is no longer pink inside, about another 4 minutes.

STUFFED BELL PEPPERS

Makes 2 servings

INGREDIENTS

Proteins:

turkey, ground, extra lean, 8 oz

Vegetables and Fruits:

bell peppers, 2 medium peppers, any color
onion, 1 small, minced
jalapeno peppers, 1/2 small pepper, seeds removed, minced finely
tomato sauce, all natural, 3/4 cup

Starch:

rice, whole grain brown or wild, 1/4 cup, raw, uncooked

Fats:

olive oil, extra virgin, 4 tsp

Seasonings:

garlic, 2 cloves, minced
cajun seasoning, 1-1/4 tsp
pepper, black, 1/4 tsp
dijon mustard, 1 tsp
vegetable broth, low sodium, 3/4 cup

INSTRUCTIONS

1. Slice peppers in half lengthwise. Remove seeds. Place on a foil-lined baking pan, with the cut side facing up.

2. Heat the olive oil in a nonstick medium skillet over medium heat. Add turkey, onion, garlic, and jalapeno pepper. Cook, stirring frequently, until the onion is slightly translucent, about 7 minutes. Add cajun seasoning, black pepper, dijon mustard, vegetable broth, and rice. Reduce to a simmer, cover, and cook for about 25 minutes.

3. Preheat oven to 400 degrees F. Let rice mixture cool, then stir in 1/2 cup tomato sauce. Fill peppers evenly with the turkey rice mixture. Top with remaining 1/4 c tomato sauce. Bake for 45 minutes.

TANDOORI-STYLE CHICKEN AND CUCUMBER PITA

Makes 2 servings

INGREDIENTS

Proteins:

yogurt, Greek, plain, nonfat, 3 oz
chicken breast, boneless, skinless, 6 oz

Vegetables and Fruits:

onion, 2 tbsp, grated
cucumbers, 1 large, sliced
tomatoes, 1 medium, sliced

Starch:

pita, whole grain, 1 pita, divided in half

Fats:

coconut oil, 4 tsp

Seasonings:

ginger, 1/2 tbsp, fresh, peeled and grated
cumin, 1/2 tsp
pepper, crushed red, 1/4 tsp
turmeric, 1/4 tsp
garlic, 2 cloves, minced

INSTRUCTIONS

1. Set aside 1 tbsp of the Greek yogurt in a small bowl.

2. Combine the remaining Greek yogurt in a large, flat bowl or resealable plastic bag with the onion, ginger, cumin, red pepper, turmeric, and garlic.

3. Add the chicken and marinate in the refrigerator for 1-2 hours, turning once.

4. Preheat a large skillet over medium heat. Add the coconut oil. When the oil becomes hot, add the chicken breast. Cook for about 10 minutes on each side, or until done. To check for doneness, pierce with a fork to make sure juices run clear.

5. Let chicken cool, then dice. Stuff evenly into pita halves, then add cucumbers and tomatoes. Top with the reserved Greek yogurt.

TOFU WITH PEPPERS AND TOMATOES OVER COUSCOUS

Makes 2 servings

INGREDIENTS

Proteins:

> **tofu**, 6 oz, extra-firm

Vegetables and Fruits:

> **tomatoes**, 2 small, diced
> **bell peppers**, 1 large, any color, chopped
> **onion**, 1 small, diced

Starch:

> **couscous, whole wheat**, 1/4 cup, instant, dry

Fats:

> **olive oil**, extra virgin, 4 tsp

Seasonings:

> **Italian herb seasoning**, salt free, dried, 2 tbsp
> **vinegar, red wine**, 2 tbsp
> **vegetable broth**, low sodium, 1 cup
> **garlic**, 2 cloves
> **pepper, black**, 1/4 tsp
> **basil**, 1/2 cup, fresh, chopped

INSTRUCTIONS

1. Squeeze tofu between towels to remove excess water. Cut into bite-sized pieces and place in a medium bowl. Add tomatoes, Italian seasoning, and balsamic vinegar and allow to marinate for 30 minutes.

2. Bring vegetable broth to boil in a small saucepan. Stir in the couscous. Remove from heat and cover. Allow couscous mixture to swell for 10 minutes.

3. Over medium-high heat in a large frying pan, heat olive oil. Add bell peppers and onion and cook until tender, about 8 minutes, stirring occasionally. Add garlic and cook for another minute, stirring constantly. Add the tofu with the marinade juices and the black pepper. Cover and reduce to simmer. Cook until heated through, about 10 minutes.

4. Serve tofu mixture over couscous and garnish with chopped basil.

TROPICAL MAHI MAHI PITA

Makes 2 servings

INGREDIENTS

Proteins:

mahi mahi, 6 oz, fillet
yogurt, Greek, plain, nonfat, 1/4 cup

Vegetables and Fruits:

limes, 1 small, juiced
mango, 1 small, diced, seeds and skin removed
pineapples, 1/3 cup, diced
jalapeno peppers, 1/4 small, seeds removed, finely minced

Starch:

pita, whole grain, 1 pita, divided into halves

Fats:

coconut oil, 2 tsp
avocado, 1/4 small, peeled and diced

Seasonings:

pepper, black, 1/2 tsp
ginger, 1/4 tsp, dried
cumin, 1/4 tsp
pepper, cayenne, 1/4 tsp
cilantro, 1/3 cup, fresh, chopped

INSTRUCTIONS

1. Season the mahi mahi on both sides with 1/4 tsp black pepper.

2. Over medium heat in a large skillet, heat the coconut oil. Add the mahi mahi and cook for about 3 minutes per side, until the fish is browned and the center just becomes opaque.

3. In a small bowl, whisk the yogurt together with the lime juice, ginger, cumin, cayenne pepper, and 1/4 tsp black pepper.

4. In a medium bowl, fold together the mango, pineapple, jalapeno, and avocado.

5. Divide the fish between the two pita halves, then add salsa and top with the yogurt mixture. Garnish with cilantro and serve.

TUNA AND COUSCOUS SALAD

Makes 2 servings

INGREDIENTS

Proteins:

tuna, chunk light, canned in water, 8 oz, drained and squeezed

Vegetables and Fruits:

bell peppers, 2 small, red
baby spinach, 2 cups, chopped
lemons, 1 small, juiced and zested

Starch:

couscous, whole wheat, 1/3 cup, dry, unprepared

Fats:

olives, 5 whole, pitted and diced
olive oil, extra virgin, 3 tsp

Seasonings:

water, 2/3 cup
garlic, 1 clove, minced
scallions, 1/2 cup, chopped
basil, 2 tbsp fresh, julienned
pepper, black, 1/4 tsp

INSTRUCTIONS

1. Bring water to boil in medium saucepan. Add couscous and reduce to simmer. Cook for 15 minutes, then drain.

2. Roast whole bell peppers over a grill or under a broiler until skin is blackened, turning once. Let cool. Slide the skin off with your fingers and dice peppers.

3. Chop or tear baby spinach. Mix in a medium bowl with olives, olive oil, lemon juice and zest, and garlic. Add tuna and hot couscous and cover for 15 minutes, stirring occasionally.

4. Mix in the scallions, basil, and black pepper just before serving.

TUNA CAKES

Makes 2 servings

INGREDIENTS

Proteins:

cottage cheese, lowfat or nonfat, 2 tbsp
tuna, chunk light, canned in water, 4 oz
egg white, 1 tbsp

Vegetables and Fruits:

bell peppers, 2 tbsp, green, diced
onion, 1 tbsp, diced finely
zucchini, 2 tbsp, shredded
jalapeno peppers, 1 tsp, diced finely
limes, 1 lime
romaine, 2 hearts

Starch:

cornmeal, whole grain, 2 tbsp

Fats:

olive oil, extra virgin, 2 tsp

Seasonings:

pepper, black, 1/4 tsp
garlic, 2 cloves, minced
basil, 2 tsp, dried
cilantro, 1/4 cup, chopped roughly

INSTRUCTIONS

1. Squeeze the diced and shredded bell peppers, onion, zucchini, and jalapeno pepper in paper towels to remove excess water. Allow cottage cheese to drain in a colander for 10 minutes. Combine vegetables and cottage cheese in a large bowl with tuna, black pepper, garlic, egg white, basil, and the juice from 1/2 of the lime. The mixture will be wet.

2. Preheat oven to 350 degrees F. Line a baking tray with parchment paper or nonstick aluminum foil. Use an ice cream scooper to scoop up balls of the mixture and drop onto the prepared baking sheet, leaving a few inches space on each side. Flatten balls gently so they form patties and dust the tops evenly with cornmeal. Bake the patties for about 20 minutes, or until cooked through.

3. Heat a skillet over medium-low heat. Add olive oil. Fry the patties in the oil, turning once, until lightly brown. Serve patties over a bed made of a romaine heart. Garnish with cilantro and squeeze remaining lime juice over all.

TUNA MELT WITH CASHEW SALAD

Makes 2 servings

INGREDIENTS

Proteins:

> **tuna, chunk light**, canned in water, 4 oz
> **natural cheese**, 3/4 oz sharp cheddar, shredded
> **yogurt, Greek**, plain, nonfat, 1-1/2 tbsp

Vegetables and Fruits:

> **baby mixed greens**, 2 cups
> **tomatoes**, 1 cup cherry

Starch:

> **bread, whole grain rye**, 2 slices

Fats:

> **olive oil**, extra virgin, 2 tsp
> **cashews**, 1 tbsp, chopped

Seasonings:

> **dijon mustard**, 1/2 tsp
> **pepper, black**, 1/4 tsp
> **celery seed**, 1/4 tsp
> **scallions**, 1 tbsp, minced finely
> **parsley**, 1 tsp, minced finely
> **vinegar, balsamic,** 1-1/2 tsp

INSTRUCTIONS

1. Preheat broiler.

2. Combine tuna, yogurt, mustard, black pepper, celery seed, scallions, and parsley in a medium bowl.

3. In a small bowl, combine olive oil and balsamic vinegar. Toss salad greens with the vinaigrette and chopped cashews.

4. Place bread on a tray 6" below the broiler heating element and toast both sides.

5. Remove from oven and spread the tuna mixture evenly onto the bread. Sprinkle the cheddar cheese on top and broil for 3-5 more minutes until the cheese has melted. Serve with salad.

TURKEY BURGERS

Makes 2 servings

INGREDIENTS

Proteins:

turkey, ground, extra lean, 8 oz

Vegetables and Fruits:

apples, 1 small, diced
onion, 1/2 small, diced
oranges, 1 small, juiced and zested
arugula, 1/2 cup leaves

Starch:

bread, whole grain wheat or multigrain, 2 slices

Fats:

olive oil, extra virgin, 4 tsp

Seasonings:

parsley, 2 tbsp, fresh, chopped
sage, 1 tsp, fresh, chopped
pepper, black, 1/4 tsp

INSTRUCTIONS

1. Preheat oven to 250 degrees F. Place bread slices on center rack and allow to dry out thoroughly, about 1 hour. Remove from oven and let cool. Pulverize in blender or food processor, or tear into very small pieces by hand to make soft breadcrumbs.

2. Over medium heat, in a large skillet heat 2 tsp olive oil. Add onion and apple and cook to soften, stirring often, about 5 minutes. Add 2 tbsp orange juice and cook till reduced by 2/3, about 2 minutes.

3. Combine ground turkey, breadcrumbs, onion-apple mixture, parsley, sage, black pepper and 1/4 tsp orange zest. Form into 2 patties.

4. Heat remaining 2 tsp of olive oil in large skillet over medium heat. Add turkey burgers. Cook about 5 minutes per side or until burgers are no longer pink in the middle.

5. Serve burgers atop arugula leaves.

TURKEY MEATLOAF

Makes 2 servings

INGREDIENTS

Proteins:

turkey, ground, extra lean, 8 oz

Vegetables and Fruits:

onion, 1 small, minced
carrots, 1 small, shredded
celery, 1 stalk, finely diced
tomato sauce, all natural, 2 tbsp

Starch:

rye flakes, whole grain, 1/4 cup

Fats:

olive oil, extra virgin, 4 tsp

Seasonings:

dijon mustard, 1 tsp
garlic, 4 cloves
pepper, black, 1/4 tsp

INSTRUCTIONS

1. Preheat oven to 350 degrees F. Toast rye flakes on a baking sheet for 5 minutes or until slightly browned.

2. Over medium heat in a small saute pan, heat olive oil. Add onion, carrots, and celery. Cook, stirring frequently, until softened and fragrant, about 10 minutes. Let cool.

3. Preheat oven to 350 degrees F. In a large bowl, mix the onion mixture, ground turkey, toasted rye flakes, dijon mustard, garlic, pepper, and tomato sauce with hands just until combined.

4. Press meat mixture into a small loaf pan. Insert a thermometer into the center of the meat and cook until it reaches 160 degrees F (about 40 minutes). Allow loaf to rest for at least 5 minutes before serving.

TURKEY SLOPPY JOES

Makes 2 servings

INGREDIENTS

Proteins:

turkey, ground, extra lean, 8 oz

Vegetables and Fruits:

onion, 1/2 small, diced
tomato sauce, all natural, 1/4 cup
apples, 1/2 small, diced

Starch:

pita, whole grain, 1 pita, halved

Fats:

olive oil, extra virgin, 2 tsp
avocado, 1/4 avocado, peeled and pitted, sliced thinly

Seasonings:

garlic, 3 cloves, diced
dijon mustard, 1 tsp
vinegar, cider, 1-1/2 tsp
chili powder, chipotle, 1/8 tsp
pepper, crushed red, 1/8 tsp

INSTRUCTIONS

1. Over medium heat in a large skillet, heat olive oil. Add onion and garlic and cook until browned, about 8 minutes, stirring frequently.

2. Add turkey and continue to saute until completely browned, about 8 more minutes.

3. Add the tomato sauce, diced apples, dijon mustard, cider vinegar, chili powder, and crushed red pepper.

4. Bring to a boil, then reduce to simmering. Continue to cook, stirring occasionally, until the sauce reduces to the consistency of a thick gravy.

5. Serve with avocado slices in pita halves.

VEGETARIAN CHILI

Makes 2 servings

INGREDIENTS

Proteins:

beans, 1/2 of a 15-1/2 oz can, kidney, reduced sodium, with liquid

Vegetables and Fruits:

onion, 1 small, diced
carrots, 1 carrots, peeled and julienned
bell peppers, 1 small, green, seeds removed, diced
celery, 1 stalk, chopped
mushrooms, 1/2 cup, fresh, chopped
tomatoes, 2 medium, diced

Starch:

corn, 3/4 cup, kernels, frozen

Fats:

olive oil, extra virgin, 2 tsp
avocado, 1/4 avocado, peeled and sliced

Seasonings:

garlic, 2 cloves, minced
chili powder, 2 tbsp
cumin, 1/2 tsp
oregano, 1 tsp, dried
basil, 1 tsp, dried

INSTRUCTIONS

1. Over medium-high heat in a medium saucepan, heat olive oil. Add onions, carrots, garlic, bell pepper, celery, and chili powder. Saute until tender, stirring occasionally, about 8 minutes.

2. Add mushrooms and cook for another 5 minutes. Add tomatoes, kidney beans with juice, corn, cumin, oregano and basil.

3. Bring to a boil, then reduce to simmer. Cook for 20 minutes, stirring occasionally.

4. Serve with avocado slices.

BREAKFAST RECIPES

ASPARAGUS-MUSHROOM MUG OMELET

Makes 2 servings

INGREDIENTS

Proteins:

eggs, 1 egg
egg whites, 1/4 cup
cottage cheese, lowfat or nonfat, 4 tbsp

Vegetables and Fruits:

asparagus, 1 cup, spears, frozen, chopped, defrosted and patted dry
mushrooms, 3/4 cup, canned, sliced, drained and patted dry
lemons, 2 tsp, juice only

Starch:

bread, whole grain rye, 2 slices

Fats:

olive oil, extra virgin, 4 tsp

Seasonings:

paprika, 1/4 tsp
pepper, black, 1/4 tsp

INSTRUCTIONS

1. Brush the insides of two microwave-safe mugs with olive oil.

2. In a medium bowl, whisk together egg, egg whites, paprika, and black pepper. Pour into mug.

3. In the same medium bowl, stir together asparagus, mushrooms, lemon juice, and cottage cheese. Pour over the egg mixture.

4. Microwave for 2 minutes. Cook for 30 seconds, then repeat as needed, until eggs are set, about 2 more minutes, depending on microwave power.

5. Serve with whole grain toast.

BANANA-WALNUT OATMEAL

Makes 2 servings

INGREDIENTS

Proteins:

> **whey protein powder**, 1/4 cup, unsweetened
> **yogurt, Greek, plain, nonfat**, 1/4 cup

Vegetables and Fruits:

> **bananas**, 1 cup, slices

Starch:

> **oats, rolled**, 1/2 cup, old-fashioned

Fats:

> **walnuts**, 4 tbsp, chopped roughly

Seasonings:

> **cinnamon**, 1 tsp
> **water**, 1 cup

INSTRUCTIONS

1. In a small saute pan over medium heat, toss walnuts until toasted and fragrant. Set aside.

2. In a medium-sized, microwave-safe bowl, combine oats, banana, cinnamon, water, and whey protein powder. Microwave on high for 3 minutes. Stir. Microwave for another 2-3 minutes, until water is absorbed. Let stand for a few minutes.

3. Stir in Greek yogurt and sprinkle walnuts on top.

BREAKFAST TORTILLA OMELET

Makes 2 servings

INGREDIENTS

Proteins:

eggs, 1 egg
egg whites, 1/3 cup
yogurt, Greek, plain, nonfat, 2 tbsp

Vegetables and Fruits:

jalapeno peppers, 1/2 pepper, seeded and diced finely
tomatoes, 1 medium, diced

Starch:

corn tortillas, whole grain, 4 tortillas, cut into strips

Fats:

olive oil, extra virgin, 4 tsp

Seasonings:

paprika, 1/4 tsp
pepper, black, 1/4 tsp
scallions, 4 scallions, sliced thinly

INSTRUCTIONS

1. Over medium-high heat in a medium saucepan, heat olive oil. Cook and stir jalapeno pepper and tortilla strips until softened, about 4 minutes.

2. Whisk eggs and egg whites with paprika and black pepper. Pour over hot skillet and top with tomatoes and scallions.

3. Turn omelet when underside begins to turn golden brown. Serve with Greek yogurt.

HASH BROWN OMELET

Makes 2 servings

INGREDIENTS

Proteins:

egg, 1 egg
egg whites, 1/2 cup

Vegetables and Fruits:

onion, 1/2 small, diced
bell peppers, 1 cup, frozen, mixed colors, strips

Starch:

potatoes, skin on, 1 small potato, shredded

Fats:

olive oil, extra virgin, 4 tsp

Seasonings:

pepper, black, 1/4 tsp
pepper, cayenne, 1/4 tsp

INSTRUCTIONS

1. Over medium-high heat in a medium saute pan, heat olive oil. Add onions and cook, stirring frequently, until they begin to soften, about 3 minutes. Add the bell pepper slices and shredded potato and continue cooking, stirring constantly, for 5 more minute

2. In a medium bowl, whisk together egg, egg whites, black and cayenne peppers. Pour into skillet.

3. Cook until bottom side of omelet is lightly browned, then flip with a spatula.

PEAR-ALMOND FRENCH TOAST

Makes 2 servings

INGREDIENTS

Proteins:

eggs, 1 egg
egg whites, 1/4 cup
yogurt, nonfat (0%) vanilla, 6 tbsp

Vegetables and Fruits:

pears, 2 small pears, cored and sliced into 1/4" slices

Starch:

bread, whole grain, 2 slices

Fats:

almonds, 4 tbsp, sliced

Seasonings:

cinnamon, 1/4 tsp, ground
ginger, 1/4 tsp, ground
vanilla extract, pure, 1/2 tsp

INSTRUCTIONS

1. Preheat oven to 350 degrees F. Toss pears with cinnamon and ginger.

2. In a shallow, medium sized bowl, whisk together egg, egg whites, 2 tbsp of vanilla yogurt, and vanilla extract.

3. In a large skillet over medium heat, toast almonds, tossing frequently, until golden brown, about 1-2 minutes. Remove from heat.

4. Dip bread slices in egg mixture, soaking to drench and turning to coat both sides.

5. Line a baking dish with parchment paper or nonstick aluminum foil. Arrange the sliced pears on the dish, then place the bread slices on top of them.

6. Bake until golden brown, or about 15-20 minutes. Use a spatula to serve pear-side up. Top with toasted almonds and drizzle with the remaining 1/4 cup of vanilla yogurt.

QUINOA PORRIDGE WITH APPLES

Makes 2 servings

INGREDIENTS

Proteins:

yogurt, nonfat (0%) vanilla, 12 oz

Vegetables and Fruits:

apples, 1 apple, small, cored and diced
raisins, 1/4 cup

Starch:

quinoa, 1/4 cup, dry, rinsed, uncooked

Fats:

walnuts, 1/4 cup, coarsely chopped

Seasonings:

water, 3/4 cup
cinnamon, 1/2 tsp
nutmeg, 1/4 tsp

INSTRUCTIONS

1. In a small saute pan over medium-high heat, toss walnuts, roasting until fragrant.

2. Bring water to boil in a medium saucepan. Stir in the quinoa, apples, and raisins and reduce to simmering. Cook until tender, about 15-20 minutes. Drain to remove any excess water. Add cinnamon and nutmeg.

3. To serve, scoop quinoa into bowls and top with vanilla yogurt and toasted walnuts.

SCRAMBLED TOFU, TOMATO AND SPINACH

Makes 2 servings

INGREDIENTS

Proteins:

tofu, 5.6 oz, firm, drained squeezed in towels, and cut into 1/2" cubes

Vegetables and Fruits:

baby spinach, 2 cups
lemons, 1 lemon, cut in half
tomatoes, 1 cup, grape, cut in half

Starch:

bread, whole grain rye, 2 pieces

Fats:

olive oil, extra virgin, 4 tsp

Seasonings:

turmeric, 1/2 tsp
pepper, black, 1/4 tsp
pepper, cayenne, 1/4 tsp
scallions, 4 scallions, sliced thinly, both white and green parts
basil, 1/2 cup, fresh, chopped

INSTRUCTIONS

1. In a medium bowl, toss together tofu, turmeric, and black and cayenne peppers.

2. Over medium-high heat in a large nonstick skillet, heat the olive oil. Add the white part of the scallions and cook about 1 minute, or until soft.

3. Add the seasoned tofu and continue to cook, stirring occasionally, until the tofu becomes lightly browned, about 5 minutes.

4. Stir in the spinach and squeeze half of the lemon over it. Stir for about a minute, until the spinach wilts.

5. Add the tomatoes and green part of the scallions and heat through for another minute or two. Garnish with the basil and serve with the other half of the lemon, cut into wedges, and a piece of toast.

SMOOTHIE BOWL WITH BERRIES

Makes 2 servings

INGREDIENTS

Proteins:

> **skim milk**, 1/2 cup
> **whey protein protein**, unsweetened, 1/4 cup
> **yogurt, nonfat (0%), vanilla**, 3 oz, frozen in an ice cube tray

Vegetables and Fruits:

> **strawberries**, 3/4 cups, frozen (can be mixed/substituted with other berries if desired)
> **bananas**, 1/2 banana, overripe, sliced and frozen

Starch:

> **oats, rolled**, 2/3 cups, old-fashioned, uncooked

Fats:

> **almonds**, 4 tbsp, chopped

Seasonings:

INSTRUCTIONS

1. Preheat oven to 350 degrees F. Mix oats and almonds together and spread on a baking sheet. Cook almonds and oats for about 10 minutes, turning occasionally, until golden brown. Remove from oven.

2. In a blender, combine skim milk, whey protein powder, strawberries, bananas, and frozen yogurt cubes.

3. Pour smoothie into a bowl and top with toasted almonds and oats.

SNACK RECIPES

BLACK BEAN DIP WITH TORTILLA CHIPS

Makes 2 servings

INGREDIENTS

Proteins:

beans, 1 cup, black, canned, reduced sodium, drained, rinsed

Vegetables and Fruits:

onion, 1 small, diced
tomatoes, 1 small, diced

Starch:

corn tortillas, whole grain, 4 tortillas

Fats:

olive oil, extra virgin, 4 tsp

Seasonings:

garlic, 1 clove, minced
cumin, 1/2 tsp
oregano, 1 tsp, fresh, chopped
chili powder, chipotle, 1/4 tsp
water, 1/2 cup
cilantro, 1 tbsp, fresh, chopped

INSTRUCTIONS

1. Preheat oven to 400 degrees F. Cut tortillas into 6 wedges each and arrange on a large baking sheet covered in aluminum foil. Bake until crisp and golden brown, about 10 minutes.

2. Over medium-high heat in a medium saucepan, heat olive oil. Add onion and cook, stirring frequently, until tender, about 8 minutes.

3. Add garlic and cook for another minute, stirring constantly. Add cumin, oregano, chili powder, beans, and water. Bring to a boil, then reduce to simmer. Cook until thickened, stirring occasionally, about 10 minutes.

4. Mash bean mixture with a food processor, blender, or potato masher.

5. Spoon tomatoes over bean mixture, garnish with cilantro, and serve with tortilla chips.

COTTAGE CHEESE CAPRESE SALAD

Makes 2 servings

INGREDIENTS

Proteins:

cottage cheese, lowfat or nonfat, 1 cup

Vegetables and Fruits:

tomatoes, 2 large, chopped

Starch:

rye crisps, whole grain, 4 crisps

Fats:

olive oil, extra virgin, 4 tsp

Seasonings:

basil, 1/4 cup, fresh, chopped
pepper, black, 1/4 tsp
vinegar, balsamic, 4 tsp

INSTRUCTIONS

1. Fold together in a large bowl the cottage cheese, tomatoes, basil, and black pepper.

2. In a small bowl, combine olive oil and balsamic vinegar.

3. Top rye crackers with cottage cheese mixture. Drizzle with olive oil and balsamic dressing.

EGGPLANT MINI PIZZAS

Makes 2 servings

INGREDIENTS

Proteins:

natural cheese, 2 oz, shredded, mozzarella

Vegetables and Fruits:

eggplant, 1/2 of a medium eggplant, sliced into 1/2" thick rounds
tomato sauce, all natural, 1/3 cup
mushrooms, 1/4 cup, fresh, sliced

Starch:

rye crisps, whole grain, 4 crisps

Fats:

olive oil, extra virgin, 4 tsp

Seasonings:

pepper, black, 1/4 tsp
Italian herb seasoning, salt free, dried, 1 tbsp
basil, 2 tbsp, fresh, chopped or torn into small pieces

INSTRUCTIONS

1. Preheat oven to 350 degrees F. Brush both sides of eggplant slices with olive oil and place on a baking sheet lined with aluminum foil or parchment paper. Sprinkle with black pepper. Bake for 8 minutes. Turn over.

2. Mix tomato sauce with Italian herb seasoning and spread atop the eggplant slices. Layer mushroom slices on top, then sprinkle shredded cheese on evenly. Top with basil.

3. Bake about 5 minutes more, or until cheese is melted. Serve with rye crisps.

MARGHERITA PITA PIZZA WITH OLIVE

Makes 2 servings

INGREDIENTS

Proteins:

natural cheese, 4 oz, mozzarella, shredded

Vegetables and Fruits:

tomatoes, 1 roma, sliced
baby spinach, 1 cup, shredded
tomato sauce, all natural, 2 tbsp

Starch:

pita, whole grain, 1 pita

Fats:

olive oil, extra virgin, 2 tsp
olives, 10 olives, sliced

Seasonings:

Italian herb seasoning, salt free, dried, 1 tsp
basil, 2 tbsp, fresh, chopped

INSTRUCTIONS

1. Preheat oven to 400 degrees F.

2. Line a baking sheet with aluminum foil. Brush both sides of pita with olive oil and place on baking sheet. Cook until slightly browned, turning once, about 8 minutes.

3. In a small bowl, combine tomato sauce and Italian herb seasoning. Add toppings to pita: sprinkle on mozzarella, then spinach, then tomato and olive slices, and then the basil.

4. Bake for another 8-10 minutes until the cheese is melted and the tomatoes and olives are soft.

NO-BAKE OATMEAL, RAISIN, AND PEANUT BUTTER BALLS

Makes 2 servings

INGREDIENTS

Proteins:

whey protein, 1/2 cup powder

Vegetables and Fruits:

raisins, 1/2 cup, chopped

Starch:

oats, rolled, 2/3 cups, old-fashioned, raw

Fats:

peanut butter, all natural, 2 tbsp

Seasonings:

orange zest, 1/2 tsp
cinnamon, 1/2 tsp
water, 2 tsp, or as much or little as needed

INSTRUCTIONS

1. Toast oats on a baking sheet in a 350 degree oven, about 10 minutes.

2. In a medium bowl, heat peanut butter until melted, about 10 seconds. Add the oats, raisins, orange zest, whey protein powder, and cinnamon. Stir to combine, adding water drop by drop as needed to make the mixture malleable.

3. Form into balls and place on a small plate. Refrigerate for about an hour.

PEAR PITA PIZZA

Makes 2 servings

INGREDIENTS

Proteins:

natural cheese, 2 oz, gorgonzola, crumbled

Vegetables and Fruits:

pears, 1 ripe, medium, cored and sliced thinly
raisins, 1/4 cup, yellow, finely chopped

Starch:

pita, whole grain, 1 pita

Fats:

olive oil, extra virgin, 2 tsp
almonds, 2 tbsp, slivered

Seasonings:

vinegar, balsamic, 1 tsp (optional)

INSTRUCTIONS

1. Preheat oven to 400 degrees F.

2. Line a baking sheet with aluminum foil. Brush pita on both sides with olive oil and place on baking sheet. Cook for 8 minutes, turning once, until slightly crisped.

3. Add toppings to pita: sprinkle on gorgonzola cheese, then pear slices and raisins, and finally the almond slivers.

4. Bake until cheese is melted and pears are soft, about 12 minutes.

5. Drizzle with balsamic vinegar before serving, if desired.

ROASTED PEACH FROZEN YOGURT WITH TOASTED NUTS AND OATS

Makes 2 servings

INGREDIENTS

Proteins:

yogurt, nonfat (0%) vanilla, 12 oz

Vegetables and Fruits:

peaches, 2 small peaches, peeled, cored, and cut into 1/2" thick slices
lemons, 1 tsp, juice only

Starch:

oats, rolled, 2/3 cup, old-fashioned, uncooked

Fats:

walnuts, 4 tbsp, chopped

Seasonings:

cinnamon, 1/2 tsp

INSTRUCTIONS

1. Preheat oven to 350 degrees F. Mix oats and walnuts together and spread on a baking sheet. Cook for about 10 minutes, turning occasionally, until golden brown. Remove from oven.

2. Toss peach slices with lemon juice. Line baking sheet with parchment paper or nonstick aluminum foil and place peach slices on it. Bake until peaches are soft and deeper in color, about 15 minutes, then remove to a bowl and cool.

3. Combine peaches with vanilla yogurt and cinnamon in a blender or food processor. Puree.

4. Freeze yogurt peach mixture until firm, about 3 hours.

5. Sprinkle toasted oats and walnuts on yogurt and serve.

ROSEMARY POTATO CHIPS WITH SPINACH DIPPING SAUCE

Makes 2 servings

INGREDIENTS

Proteins:

cottage cheese, lowfat or nonfat, 1 cup

Vegetables and Fruits:

spinach, 1 package, frozen, chopped, 10 oz, defrosted

Starch:

potatoes, skin on, 1 small

Fats:

almonds, 2 tbsp, slivers
olive oil, extra virgin, 2 tsp

Seasonings:

garlic powder, 1/2 tsp
pepper, black, 1/4 tsp
rosemary, 1 tsp, dry, crushed

INSTRUCTIONS

1. In a small saute pan over medium heat, toast almonds, stirring constantly, for about 1 minute.

2. In a medium bowl, combine cottage cheese, spinach, garlic powder, and black pepper.

3. Preheat oven to 375 degrees F.

4. Slice potatoes as thinly and evenly as possible. For best results, use a mandoline.

5. Toss potatoes in a medium bowl with oil and rosemary.

6. Line a baking sheet with aluminum foil or parchment paper. Place potatoes on sheet and bake for 15-20 minutes, checking frequently, removing individual chips as soon as they are golden brown.

SKILLET APPLE CRISP

Makes 2 servings

INGREDIENTS

Proteins:

yogurt, nonfat (0%) vanilla, 12 oz

Vegetables and Fruits:

apples, 2 small, cored and sliced into 1/2" slices

Starch:

oats, rolled, 2/3 cup, old-fashioned, uncooked

Fats:

coconut oil, 4 tsp

Seasonings:

cinnamon, 1 tsp

INSTRUCTIONS

1. In a medium bowl, toss oats and 1/2 tsp cinnamon. Use hands to mix in 2 tsp coconut oil until mixture is somewhat crumbly.

2. Over medium-high heat in a medium sized skillet, heat remaining 2 tsp coconut oil. Add apples and stir until crisp-tender, about 5-6 minutes.

3. Stir in the remaining 1/2 tsp cinnamon.

4. Pour the oats into the pan, reduce heat to medium-low, and cover. Cook until oats are tender, stirring occasionally, 10-15 minutes.

5. Serve warm apple crisp over vanilla yogurt.

SWEET POTATO FRIES WITH CUCUMBER DILL DIPPING SAUCE

Makes 2 servings

INGREDIENTS

Proteins:

yogurt, Greek, plain, nonfat, 12 oz

Vegetables and Fruits:

cucumbers, 1 shredded

Starch:

sweet potatoes, 1 small (5" long)

Fats:

olive oil, extra virgin, 4 tsp

Seasonings:

dill, 1 tbsp, fresh, finely chopped
pepper, black, 1/4 tsp
pepper, cayenne, 1/4 tsp

INSTRUCTIONS

1. Prepare the dipping sauce by combining Greek yogurt, shredded cucumber, dill, and black pepper in a small bowl.

2. Preheat oven to 450 degrees F.

3. Cut the sweet potato in half lengthwise, then slice each half into 3 spears. Place spears on a baking sheet lined with aluminum foil and toss with olive oil. Sprinkle with cayenne pepper.

4. Bake for 15 minutes, then turn. Cook for another 10 minutes or until browned lightly.

5. Serve with cucumber dill dipping sauce.

ZUCCHINI PARMESAN CHEESE CHIPS

Makes 2 servings

INGREDIENTS

Proteins:

natural cheese, 2 oz, parmesan, fresh, grated

Vegetables and Fruits:

zucchini, 1 medium, sliced into 1/4" thick slices

Starch:

bread, whole grain rye, 2 slices

Fats:

olive oil, extra virgin, 4 tsp

Seasonings:

Italian herb seasoning, salt free, dried, 2 tsp

INSTRUCTIONS

1. Place bread slices directly on rack in oven preheated to 250 degrees F. Allow to cook until crisp and dried out, about 1 hour. Use a food processor, blender, or chef's knife to chop into coarse breadcrumbs.

2. Increase oven temperature to 450 degrees F. In a small bowl, combine the breadcrumbs, parmesan, and Italian seasoning mix. Cover a baking sheet with nonstick aluminum foil.

3. In a medium bowl, toss the zucchini slices with the olive oil. Dip the tops of the slices into the parmesan bread crumb mixture and place, bottom-side down, onto the baking sheet.

4. Bake until crisp and brown on top, about 30 minutes. Best when served immediately.